AF479078

God and Human Freedom

AMERICAN UNIVERSITY STUDIES

SERIES VII

THEOLOGY AND RELIGION

VOL. 354

This book is a volume in a Peter Lang monograph series.
Every volume is peer reviewed and meets
the highest quality standards for content and production.

PETER LANG

New York • Bern • Frankfurt • Berlin
Brussels • Vienna • Oxford • Warsaw

TONY KIM

God and Human Freedom

A Kierkegaardian Perspective

PETER LANG
New York • Bern • Frankfurt • Berlin
Brussels • Vienna • Oxford • Warsaw

Library of Congress Cataloging-in-Publication Data

Kim, Tony.
God and human freedom: a Kierkegaardian perspective / Tony Kim.
pages cm. — (American University studies VII. Theology and religion; Vol. 354)
Includes bibliographical references and index.
1. Kierkegaard, Søren, 1813–1855. 2. Liberty. 3. Philosophical theology.
4. Liberty—Religious aspects—Christianity. 5. God (Christianity). I. Title.
B4378.L53K56   233'.7—dc23   2015008445
ISBN 978-1-4331-3064-9 (hardcover)
ISBN 978-1-4539-1595-0 (e-book)
ISSN 0740-0446

Bibliographic information published by **Die Deutsche Nationalbibliothek**.
Die Deutsche Nationalbibliothek lists this publication in the "Deutsche
Nationalbibliografie"; detailed bibliographic data are available
on the Internet at http://dnb.d-nb.de/.

Cover art by Noble Aurelius Micah Kim

The paper in this book meets the guidelines for permanence and durability
of the Committee on Production Guidelines for Book Longevity
of the Council of Library Resources.

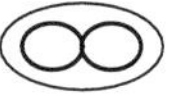

TABLE OF CONTENTS

· 1 ·

INTRODUCTION

The God-Freedom Relation

The question concerning the relation between God and human freedom in Kierkegaard is a difficult one. The reason is due to his emphatic focus on freedom. Some see his view as affirming total absence of divine constraint in human life.

For example, a Kierkegaard scholar, Louis Pojman, claims Kierkegaard is a strict proponent of human freedom and sees faith as something which is "essentially active and experienced as a result of one's willful choice of action."[1] He writes:

> Although Kierkegaard is not always as lucid as he could be in these discussions of faith/belief (*Tro*), the context usually makes the concept tolerably clear. Most of what he says I take to be insightful and plausible; however, there is one place where I think Kierkegaard's theory bears especially close scrutiny. I refer his doctrine of *volitionalism*: the thesis that we *can* attain beliefs by willing to have them, and that we ought to attain some beliefs in this manner.[2]

In Pojman's view, Kierkegaard thinks of human will as that which independently achieves religious faith without dependence on God.

In this book, I will exam the problem of God-freedom relation in Kierkegaard. Contrary to his critics, such as Pojman and others, I will argue Kierkegaard is not a strict voluntarist but acknowledges the absoluteness and the initiative of the transcendent over and against human life. Specifically, I will argue that his position is one of both synthesis and antithesis. It is former in that he acknowledges the interaction between the two; it is latter in that God's absoluteness superimposes itself on all that is human. I will add his view of the Incarnation—absolute paradox—plays a central role in the concept of the relation as one of absolute distinction and historical unity.

The Incarnation as the Starting Point

Using the Incarnation as a starting point for his God-freedom argument—as a both synthetic and antithetic historical-religious phenomenon—Kierkegaard employs the relation between God's revelation (Incarnation) and human understanding to show that paradoxical nature. According to him, the paradox of the Incarnation forever constitutes an opposition to human reason. Our natural reason, he says, cannot logically grasp the transcendent meaning of the Incarnation from any historical standpoint. Rather than subjecting to philosophical analysis, the incarnation necessitates appropriation and decision. Let me explain.

Kierkegaard believes when God created humanity he gave them freedom. That means he refrains from asserting complete dominance. However, God's restraint of dominance should not to be taken in the absolute sense. As emphatic and protective as he is over our freedom, Kierkegaard does not lack firmness when it comes to expressing what he believes is God's true intent behind creation: to reveal a single vestige of redemption. While not dis-acknowledging it, he sees freedom as summoned towards God's theological objective. There is no singular rational capacity which transcends that initiative.[3]

But, there is irony. Being rooted in God's creational origin we nonetheless play the role of historically determining existence with given scientific/rational/existential conditions. Given God's absolute determination of human life, our final or future destiny—resting upon God's inanimate or non-perceived conditions and purpose or will that at any time may override those of a person—the fact is one must act. How then do we reconcile that contradiction between God's absoluteness and human will?

First, Kierkegaard does not absolutize history. He does not form a singular unity of God and the world. He does not justify history's intelligent force as that which transcendently unifies the world with the divine. He concurs history is a process in which human beings determine their choices and relation with God and others. History is formed through interaction between God and humanity. "The paradox of faith is that the individual is higher than the universal, that the individual determines his relation to the universal by his relation to the absolute, not his relation to the absolute by his relation to the universal."[4]

He admits: "The paradox [Incarnation] can also be expressed by saying that there is an absolute duty toward God; for in this relationship of duty the individual as an individual stands related absolutely to the absolute."[5] Declaring a qualitative distinction between God (absolute) and humanity (historical) he establishes an historical axiom of our moral duty towards God.

Over and against philosophical systems of Spinoza, Hegel and others which transcendentally idealize the world, Kierkegaard maintains God's absoluteness over and against humanity without disparaging their historical unity. The given principle of absolute distinction and historical unity between God and humanity in Kierkegaard then serves as the framework of our argument.[6]

Kierkegaard rejects acknowledging God's absoluteness disparages our freedom. He rejects affirming freedom entails human autonomy. He asserts neither necessity nor autonomy. Our choice, he says, is neither solely self-determining nor solely necessitated. It is simultaneously both. Indeed our choice is both a deliberated and determined action. But it is a choice made in neglect of rationality. Human choices are unconsciously determined.

In the next section, we will show how he validates that argument. We will achieve that by means of giving textual proof and a philosophical argument for self-transcendence.

Freedom and Self-Transcendence

According to Kierkegaard, human beings express subjective transcendental interest in the transcendent. In transcending finite existence, they express metaphysical interests of infinite possibilities, such as God's existence and eternal happiness.

But for Kierkegaard, the foundation of human happiness lies outside the world, outside the human subject. At the same time he acknowledges the objectivity of that foundation, namely the transcendent, and avails eternal happiness as the object of our historical pursuit. What he offers as the way is an ascent from the historical to the eternal.

How that works is that the ascent or leap neglects the present by discrediting all rational arguments that fail to absolutely qualify the truth (God) of eternal happiness. In asking: "[How] does the existence of the god emerge?" He answers "let go" [*jeg slipper*].

> So long as I am holding on to the [rational] demonstration, that is, continue to be one who is demonstrating, the existence does not emerge, if for no other reason than that I am in the process demonstrating it, but when I let go of the demonstration, the existence is there.

Here, one must be careful as not to think the idea of letting go denotes dominance of human freedom or will over and against any and every possible restraining opposition, including God. Instead it points out discrediting rational proofs facilitates resolving rational dichotomy between God and self-transcendence or freedom. It objectifies the transcendent and transports happiness to human subject.

Objectifying the transcendent and thus gaining happiness takes place through mediating the transcendent. That mediation is imposed solely by the transcendent.[7] That does not mean our choices are undermined. That is because our relation with God is one of both polarity and unity where polarity depicts contradiction between God and human will. As one theologian acutely puts it:

> No one ever treats a man either as a mere locus of a series of contingent actions or as a mechanism in which calculable effects follow from calculated causes. Man always considers man—including himself—in terms of a unity of freedom and destiny. The fact that finite man is threatened with the loss of one side of the polarity—and consequently with the loss of the other, since loss of either side destroys the polarity as a whole—only confirms the essential character of the ontological structure.[8]

The question concerning God-freedom relation as both polarity and unity will be further discussed later.

For now, we must turn our attention to two eminent thinkers from the modern period who, contrary to Kierkegaard, championed the cause of freedom by redefining it as an existentially autonomous concept: they are Immanuel Kant and Martin Heidegger. The intent is to show the relevance of their shared emphasis on freedom with Kierkegaard, and to demonstrate their significant differences. As much as he anchors human life on freedom as do others, Kierkegaard also employs that point to disqualify sufficiency of freedom and points to necessity of the transcendent. I will give their analysis and render a Kierkegaardian critique.

· 2 ·

MODERN CONCEPTS OF FREEDOM

Kant's Critique of Reason as a Prologemena to Future Study of Human Freedom

The problem of God and freedom has always been in the fore of the history of philosophy, especially in the modern period. Anthropologically, the problem touches on the main crust of what it means to be human. For Kierkegaard, the meaning of life derives from our relation to the divine. And the moral objectivity of our experience is true in our relation to the transcendent. And our freedom is rooted in that context of our relation with and to the eternal.

But there are those who demonstrate different views. In this part of the book, we will discuss one of those views, which is found in Immanuel Kant. First, we will analyze his philosophical anthropology with intent to show the lacking theological elements in his thinking. Second, we will nonetheless show the transparent shadow of Kant's philosophy in Kierkegaard. Our discussion will make it evident how Kant's concept of God-world relation serves as a platform for Kierkegaard's own take on the problem concerning the God-freedom relation as one of absolute distinction and historical relation.

Kant's view of freedom represents a self-determining quality. He calls freedom an "absolute self-activity." According to Kant, freedom is: "the 'power' of man to determine himself from himself."[1] Interestingly, according to German philosopher Martin Heidegger, Kant is the first philosopher to connect the problem of human freedom with metaphysics. "Kant," says Heidegger, "occupies a distinctive position in the history of the problem of freedom." He explains: "Kant brings the problem of freedom for the first time explicitly into a radical connection with the fundamental problems of metaphysics."[2]

Kant's discussion of freedom in connection to the problem of reason is mainly found in his work *Critique of Pure Reason*. There he demonstrates how philosophy plays an important role in depicting human freedom as autonomous and independent from God and nature.

In his book he argues human knowledge is made up of two fundamental components: "matter" and "form." Matter is "whatever corresponds to sensation" and form is an "appearance."[3] Matter "signifies the determinable as such" and the form "signifies its determination," an appearance of an object. Those two components essentially constitute the basic structure of an object.

An object is subject to both of what he calls empirical and ideal appropriation. Concerning an object, Kant claims: "It is wholly contradictory and impossible that a concept should be produced completely *a priori* and yet refer to an object, if that concept neither were itself included in the concept of possible experience nor consisted of elements of a possible experience."[4] In other words, an object is experienced as a totality of its real and the ideal components. We gain knowledge of an object as it conforms to the understanding's different categories or a priori concepts, which then dispenses the data for various functions. The understanding gives out knowledge from the sensory data by the rational categories it contains. Those categories extract the data from an object and appropriate its formal (physical) meaning. Simultaneously, the understanding appropriates its concept which lies beyond the object's empirical perception. That process is called metaphysics.

Metaphysics attempts to gain ideal knowledge of objects conceptually in their a priori state or condition, the *Dingen-Sachen-an-sich* (things-in-themselves). It is simply an attempt at gaining the object's a priori meaning which bears the reality of the object's ideal meaning beyond the empirical. As a noted scholar, Stephen Körner, helpfully puts:

> The structure of objective experience…this account certainly implies the existence of an unknown and unknowable X which 'affects' our senses with something which is 'transformed' into objective and scientific reality by being 'subjected' to certain forms—on the one hand to the forms of perception, and on the other to the form of the understanding, the latter being simply the sum total of *synthetic a priori* principles.[5]

Some epistemological categories, such as perception and judgment, apply to the objects of the *phenomenal*.[6] He calls them the objects of sensibility or empirical experience. Others are metaphysical categories which correspond to the *noumenal* (things as such and in themselves). Whereas one has access to the phenomenal, the access to the noumenal is prohibited. "The objects of experience,' says Kant, "are the only objects which we can know…and the categories cannot be applied to anything outside empirical experience. What is certain is there is an unknown or unknowable world outside the physical. According to Körner:

> We are committed, according to Kant, to the thesis *that* there are things in themselves although we cannot know what they are. Indeed, as has been pointed out by Schopenhauer, we cannot even properly speak of things in themselves or the thing in itself, since in doing so we seem *ex hypothesis* cannot come under any Category. Kant calls the things in themselves 'noumena' because they are entities of the understanding to which no objects of experience can ever correspond, and contrasts them with 'phenomena' which are or can be objects of experience.[7]

The objects of the unknown (noumenal) include the transcendent. It, however, remains a negative concept by not yielding to empirical experience.[8] The transcendent is a "limiting concept in so far as it is not an object of our sense-perception."[9] It does not correspond to rational categories in any other manner.[10] "It carries no metaphysical commitments with it further than the concept of the phenomenon."[11]

How Kant justifies freedom (and God and immortality for that matter, the three basic ideal or metaphysical questions for him) then is on the basis of moral experience. While Kant rejects positive access of the noumenal, he claims its existence can be morally postulated. According to Kant: "Morality necessarily presupposes freedom (in the strictest sense) as a property of our will; for morality adduces a priori, as data of reason, original practical principles residing in reason, and these principles would be absolutely impossible without the presuppositions of freedom."[12] The noumenal is implied in the will as properties which belong to that will.

In his *Critique of Practical Reason*, Kant claims our practical reason contains "principles…which contain a general determination of the will."[13] In performing a moral act one becomes conscious of freedom as a transcendent cause. The practical reason or the self-determining will is predicated upon what he calls the categorical imperative of the moral law. According to him, "The 'categorical ought,' a will pure and practical of itself which contains the supreme condition, in accordance with reason, is roughly like the way in which understanding signify nothing but lawful form in general."[14]

According to Kant, the moral law residing in every person dictates their actions. He asserts: "The universal principle of morality is the ground of all actions of rational beings, just as the laws of nature is the ground of all appearances."[15] And all our actions are judged on the basis of their conformity or inconformity to those moral imperatives.

Incidentally there are two forms of imperatives: Hypothetical and categorical. The former assumes a superior end which it desires to achieve. For instance, if the perceived end is happiness, then the imperative is hypothetical (because it is not yet achieved) and the will reveals proper means towards achieving that end. The latter, categorical imperative, lays claim for its universal validity.[16] In other words, it justifies its own ground in and for itself. Its aim is nothing other than itself. The ultimate good resides in itself as "the form of the will," and "the law of its lawfulness."[17] It is the ultimate good and the law in itself.

Within that order of imperatives Kant renders logic: the imperative—of the moral law—compels us to hypothesize freedom. It "compels us to assume such a being [freedom] as a subjectively necessary hypothesis."[18] That hypothesis conversely shows the sufficiency of the moral principle, which carries the ethical task towards none other than the world's utopian establishment.

> The proposition that the human race has always progressively improved and will continue to develop in the same way is not just a well-meant saying to be recommended for practical purposes. Whatever unbelievers may say, it is tenable within the most strictly theoretical context. And if one considers not only the events which may happen within a particular nation, but also their repercussions upon all the nations of the earth which might gradually begin to participate in them, a view opens up to the unbounded future. [19]

Hence the world according to Kant is an ongoing evolution of development and progress. Its cosmic destiny is to become a perfect humanity of eternal continuance.[20] In advocating ethical naturalism he informs of our ethical values which culminate as a perfect society.

Adding to Kant's assertion, a 20th century American theologian, Reinhold Neibhur, says Kant's philosophy played a major role in shaping modern thinking. According to Neibhur, Kant's thought greatly influenced Christian theology in the nineteenth century and politics in the twentieth century. In theology, says Neibhur, we saw a strong and fast resurgence of liberal theology which announced rational absurdity of God's immanence in and involvement with the world. In rejecting God's presence in the world, liberal theology rejected Christ's deity, transmuting it into a mere historic figure who "incarnates values worthy of our highest devotion."[21] In politics, the society witnessed the coming of a post-Kantian era of naturalism which embarked on Kant's utopian concept rooted in humanistic ethics of freedom (over and against the opposing supernatural ethics of Christian faith).[22]

> A thing is under the order of nature insofar as its existence or its alteration is sufficiently grounded in the forces of nature. For this is requisite first, that the force of nature be the efficient cause, and second, that the way in which the force of nature is directed toward production of this effect is itself sufficiently grounded in a rule of natural efficacy.[23]

The origin of Kant's ethical naturalism can be traced back to the time of Copernican revolution. According to a Swiss theologian, Karl Barth, the Enlightenment bore an ironic effect on philosophy. Instead of bringing humility, it created pride in human thinking. He writes:

> Eighteenth-century man was the man who could no longer remain ignorant of the significance of the fact that Copernicus and Galileo were right, that this vast and rich earth of his, the theatre of his deeds was not the centre of the universe, but a grain of dust amid countless others in this universe, and who clearly saw the consequences of all this. What did this really apocalyptic revolution in his picture of the universe mean for man? An unprecedented and boundless humiliation of man? No, said the man of the eighteenth century, who was not the first to gain this knowledge, but certainly the first to realize it fully and completely; no, man is all the greater for this, man is in the centre of all things, in a quite different sense, too, for he was able to discover this revolutionary truth by his own resources and to think it abstractly, again to consider and penetrate a world which had expanded overnight into infinity—and without anything else having changed, without his having to pay for it in any way…. It is paradoxical and yet it is a fact that the answer to his humiliation was those philosophical systems of rationalism, empiricism and skepticism which made men even more self-confident. The geocentric picture of the universe was replaced as a matter of course by the anthropocentric.[24]

As a result philosophy's emphasis turns from God and nature to reason. Humanity becomes the center of the universe. As one philosopher keenly notes:

Kant's enlightened emphasis on the use of reason is 'autonomous' inasmuch as it serves to challenge any subservience of reason to religion or revelation. In a sense Kant's critical philosophy severely curtailed the power of reason. Yet he did not bring reason into subservience to anything other than itself.[25]

Kant's Influence on Kierkegaard and Kierkegaard's Critique of Kant

Like Kant, Kierkegaard demonstrates freedom in the negative. Like his predecessor, Kant, Kierkegaard sees God-humanity relation as one of absolute distinction which puts barrier to the noumenal, and the transcendent for that matter. Freedom in Kant as a negative concept is in concordance with the fact that the mind does not provide necessary conditions to knowing freedom, the concept of which is pure and can only be determined by virtue of knowing its content a priori through transcendental deduction.[26] All of this is of course laid out so that the ultimate source of a priori concepts must be determined by the rational power contained in our reason or understanding.

But, contrary to Kant, Kierkegaard offers a different alternative: revelation. Kant's transcendental deduction which finds origin in human reason, hence conveying an anthropological perspective on such beings as God, freedom, immortality and so, Kierkegaard defines those concepts as an effect of God's divine cause, namely his revelation or grace. Whereas Kant places hypothetical correlation between God and humanity by virtue of speculative ethics on the basis of human actions, Kierkegaard religiously confirms the relation between the two of their historical relation.

His intent is to explain the historical or natural matter of the relation between God and humanity. Kant's transcendental deduction leaves the objective validity of the noumenal objects such as God vague since he believes there is no way of proving the truth of their being. What he calls pure concepts of principles of pure understanding is a law to itself which cannot be determined since they have "basis completely a priori in the understanding."[27] But Kierkegaard's view is such that the only logical solution to the objective validity of our transcendental experience of the noumenal, such as God and so one is to do it biblically. He reasons that revelation is consistent with human experience. It is the most consistent basis for our experience of the noumenal since our experience of knowledge of the transcendent is one in which a way of knowing God is bestowed by God on human beings.

Unlike Kant, Kierkegaard does not define noumenal objects speculatively. Instead he admits their reality by affirming the truth of their experience. For Kierkegaard, the objective validity of the noumenal does not require a priori investigation of those objects. It is determined by the legitimacy of the experience which self-determines its reality. Furthermore that self-determining character of our experience of the noumenal has its origin in the transcendent. That concept also posits in our understanding a life as possessing a self-determining quality. In other words, among those mixed concepts contained in the understanding is one which affirms the truth of our transcendent experience of the noumenal. It affirms God is the source of our knowledge and the world is the recipient of his truth.

This, then, brings us to an important but polemical topic concerning Kierkegaard's doctrine of natural proofs.

According to Kierkegaard, all natural or rational proofs of God's existence are meaningless: they simply beg the question as to whether God truly exists. In other words those arguments do not give absolute certainty (*a la* Kant). But those arguments, says Kierkegaard, nonetheless support the truth of God's existence. Although he does not address the matter specifically, he certainly appeals to the plausibility of God's being as it yields to our transcendental perception as an object of existential or life experience.

And the necessary condition of the knowledge of the transcendent is grace or revelation. By grace God is made an "unavoidable presence." Whereas Kant grounds reason's ideal structure in our natural thinking, Kierkegaard places its connection to the transcendent. According to Kierkegaard, the transcendent is the absolute ground of all spatial and temporal properties, including reason.

The origin of a priori forms, says Kierkegaard, cannot be situated in space and time as Kant asserts. The reason is that raises the problem of objectivity of the transcendent and reason's lack of solution.

Again, the problem in Kant's transcendental deduction is the ambiguity of the ideal. That ambiguity results from grounding "a priori origin of the spatial and temporal aspects of presentations in sensibility." For Kierkegaard, the a priori forms of spatial and temporal aspects refer to the transcendent, which is the origin of human cognition. He disparages rational arguments which make inference to God's existence and offers the alternative of revelation/ grace over and against rationality.

Despite Kant's influence on his thinking, Kierkegaard still casts a different view of the transcendent. Unlike Kant, who disparages the objectivity of the noumenal or ideal, Kierkegaard admits the facticity of the transcendent who is historically encountered.

The concept which is used to reflect that encounter is "dialectic." He declares human freedom, and rationality for that matter, combine both the ontic and the ideal aspects. Our freedom is contingent in that God is its origin.

According to philosopher Anthony Rudd, Kierkegaard's philosophical approach to the problem of freedom is such that the effort attempts to save its spiritual meaning. Kierkegaard, says Rudd, rescues "ethical and religious concepts from their abuse in abstract speculation," and returns "them to the contexts of ethical and religious existence where they have their meaning."[28]

Rudd states Kierkegaard reminds us what we already know but have missed with respect to freedom. "Kierkegaard has no body of philosophical doctrine to teach us; rather, he wants to remind us of what we already in a sense know, but have come to overlook in our enthusiasm to transcend the contexts of personal, ethical existence, and become 'objective' namely that the concept of human freedom is such that it opposes itself as a metaphysical problem and sheds a new light in the existential sphere."[29] That means Kierkegaard sees existence from both a subjective and objective standpoint. Not only does he acknowledge the rationality of God's being but also our inward affirmation of his existence.

Apparently, both Kant and Kierkegaard perceive the qualitative distinction between God and humanity. But in Kierkegaard's case, that distinction is comparable whereas in Kant it is not. That is, God's being subjects to historical measure. As Rudd keenly observes:

> For Kierkegaard, the notion that we can come to see things as God does by abstracting from our subjectivity is a huge error. The attempt to do so leads only—when it is clearly thought through—to skepticism and, when it is not, to the utter confusion of 'pure thought.' We cannot form any conception of how the world is, as a system, for God. We can only know how it seems to us from our very finite perspectives within it, and our efforts at abstraction merely take us further away from reality, rather than closer to it. The notion of the way the world is to God is, therefore, for Kierkegaard a limit-concept, akin—closely akin, I would say—to Kant's 'thing-in-itself.' It is something we can think up to, not something we can think with.[30]

Unlike Kant—who denies the historical connection between God and the world—Kierkegaard affirms it. Not only does he acknowledge their historical relation, but wholly grounds our existence in the transcendent.

With respect to our freedom, that means Kierkegaard's own concept entails a possibility of a very different form: it is both authentic and inauthentic.

Freedom is authentic in carrying the possibility of self-determination. It is in-authentic insofar as God's supreme authority takes precedence over humanity with a definite control. According to Rudd:

> Although it is plausible to suppose that indeterminism is a necessary condition for free will, it is not in itself a sufficient one. To say that my action was uncaused is not to say that I did it. From the objective point of view, actions are simply events which happen—whether deterministically, probabilistically, or randomly—but they cannot be thought of as being done by anyone.[31]

He goes on to say:

> If Kierkegaard is right and we cannot really hold on to such an objective view, then there is no bar to our seeing action, as we do in fact see it—subjectively. From the subjective point of view, we do—at least some of the time—choose freely. We do not normally assume either that our decisions are all predetermined, or that they are wholly random. We cause them to happen, and we do so for reasons.[32]

In Rudd's view, to which I am sympathetic, Kierkegaard neither advocates determinism nor necessity. He observes its limitation and offers the only solution of reconciling its double quality as a positive-negative synthesis.

> The *existential* problem of reconciling freedom and necessity is, in a sense, *the* crucial philosophical issue with which Kierkegaard was concerned—and it is more than just a philosophical issue. How can we reconcile, within human life, our limitations, our finitude? At the start of *Sickness Unto Death*, Kierkegaard gives his definition of self-hood as 'synthesis of the infinite and the finite, of the temporal and the eternal, of freedom and necessity.' In each of those pairs, one element stands for our limitedness, one for our ability to transcend our limits. Kierkegaard does not identify the true self with either transcendence or imminence, but with their synthesis (Both-And, in this case, not Either-Or!).[33] One aspect of this synthesis is the reconciliation of freedom and necessity.

The intent behind his claim of synthesis is to situate its mystery in God as the origin. He goes beyond Kant in asserting that in our a priori or ideal judgment about God we remove the condition of space and time from its intuition. But we do not deny God in time for "temporality is the time of grace" just as life is the space of grace.[34]

Now we turn to another thinker whose philosophical thought bears much importance on our discussion. He is a German philosopher named Martin Heidegger. Just as with Kant, the significance of Heidegger's philosophy lies in his relegation of Kierkegaard's concept of freedom to the realm of human autonomy. The problem which is raised here is despite stealing the concept from Kierkegaard—in order to trace its origin back to the natural world of humanity—he fails in reconciling the positive and the negative aspects of freedom.

Henceforth, we will offer a critique of Heidegger's concept of freedom. We will approach the problem within his ontological concept of Being from angles of both the objective and the subjective. Our goal is to give a religious interpretation of Kierkegaard's concept of being against the Heideggerian concept of freedom as an absolute autonomy which attacks Kierkegaard's construction of being in the context of our finitude and infinity.

Heidegger's Concept of Freedom
and a Kierkegaardian Critique

In Heidegger's ontology of being, which according to a critic is "implicit but undeveloped in Kierkegaard's description of human rationality," there is an important problem which surrounds his understanding of being or freedom: its absolute independence from God and history.[35]

Heidegger's method of answering the question of being is to do it in its totality. He does it from the standpoint of dismissing the objectivity of the transcendent in the world and human experience. In his *The Essence of Freedom: An Introduction to Philosophy*, he writes: "The question concerning human freedom, namely that it leads into the totality of beings, marks it out as a specifically philosophical question." He states:

> If every scientific question and every science as such are in their essence restricted to a region, and if the question concerning human freedom in its proper meaning forces us into the totality of beings as such, then this question cannot be a scientific one. For not only in a quantitative but also in a qualitative sense, no science has the breadth of horizon to encompass the unitary whole which is intended (albeit unclearly and indefinitely) by the question of freedom.[36]

Admittedly, for Heidegger the question of freedom intends to stress its total independence. Freedom, he declares, "primarily refers to a person's autonomy." "Freedom," he announces, "is freedom from…" It "involves the denial of dependence on something else."[37]

He introduces two types of freedom: positive and negative. The positive has its own origin. It is exactly the opposite of the negative freedom. It contains the idea of "toward-which" rather than "away-from," an idea which negative freedom denotes. It means "being free for…, being open *for*…, thus *oneself* being open *for*…, allowing *oneself* to be determined through…, determining oneself to…" It means to "determine one's own action purely through *oneself* to give to oneself the law for one's action."[38]

Negative freedom is interpreted by admitting what one is independent from and how that independence is to be understood.[39] Here, a few points must be mentioned. First, freedom in general is disconnected from nature or the world. "Freedom from…is *independence from nature*. Human action as such is not primarily caused by natural processes; it is not bound by the lawfulness of natural processes and their necessity."[40] Heidegger declares:

> This independence from nature can be grasped in a more essential way by reflecting that the inner decision and resolve of man is in a certain respect independent of the necessity which resides in human fortunes. From what was said above we could call this independence from nature and history an independence from the 'world,' where the latter is understood as the unitary totality of history and nature.[41]

Second, freedom excludes human beings' historical relation to the transcendent in Heidegger. "Freedom means independence from God." It is "autonomy in relation to God." "For only if there is such autonomy can man take up a relationship to God." Only then," he declares, "can *he* seek and acknowledge God, hold to God and take upon *himself* the demands of God." "All such being toward God," he says, "would be in principle impossible if there is no possibility of turning away from already presupposing a certain independence from and freedom in relation to God." Hence it "amounts to independence of man from world and God."[42]

> So when we treat of the essence of human freedom, albeit as understood only in this negative way, i.e. when we really reflect upon this double independence, we must necessarily keep in mind that *from which* man is independent. *World and God* are not just accidentally or contingently represented in the *negative concept of freedom*, but are *essentially included* in it. If negative freedom is the topic, then world and God necessarily belong to the topic as the 'from what' of independence. But world and God together constitute the totality of what is.[43]

Heidegger's above account with respect to freedom is an "exemplification of indifference" towards God and nature. They are cutting words of atheism and a promotion of human autonomy. This is further exemplified below:

> Not only does the question concerning the essence of freedom not limit our considerations to a particular domain, it *removes limits*; instead of limiting the inquiry it

broadens it. But, in this we are not setting out from a particular to arrive at its universality. For world and God are not the universal over against man as a particular. Man is not a particular instance of God in the way that the alpine rose is a particular instance of the essence of plant or Aeschylus's *Prometheus* a particular instance of tragedy. The removal of limits leads us into the totality of beings, i.e. world and God, in the midst of which man himself is situated, and in such a way that he stands in a relationship to world and God. It thus becomes completely clear: *the question concerning the essence of human freedom relates neither to a particular nor to a universal.* This question is different to every kind of *scientific* question, which is always confined to a particular domain and inquires into the particularity of a universal. With the question of freedom we leave behind us, or better, we do not at all enter into, everything and anything of a regional character.[44]

Heidegger's atheist account of freedom poses a problem for Kierkegaard: the concept does not objectify being genuinely. It does not acknowledge freedom's temporal character. Heidegger removes freedom's temporality and incorporates the pretense of its autonomy over and against the world and the transcendent. Freedom is at the core of all that is.

Unlike Heidegger, Kierkegaard sees freedom at the core of all that becomes. For him the essence of freedom is becoming. As one scholar, Michael Wyschogrod, correctly points out, Kierkegaard, unlike Heidegger and others, does not fail to admit freedom's temporal nature. According to Wyschogrod: "In granting full ontological status to the achievement of the moment, Kierkegaard places an emphasis upon becoming which is never lost. Becoming, in various senses of the word, becomes the central task of man in his existential situation."[45] He further states:

> What Kierkegaard has done by this argument is to establish freedom at the very core of all that becomes and, since for man everything becomes, at the core of everything. This is carried so far that even the necessity of the past is denied. Since the past, too, has become, it, too, must have come into being freely and the fact that it is now in the past adds no new necessity to it, at least as far as the 'how' of its happening is concerned. For, argues Kierkegaard, if the past was necessary, then the future is necessary also because there is no way of ascribing freedom to the future without ascribing it to the past.[46]

But, Heidegger's account exudes the opposite. Rather than ascribing human choices as temporal determinations, they determine what is already given as possibilities of choice. Freedom determines the action in a situation in which all the factors that contribute to the result are given.[47] Rather than giving ourselves to the possibilities of actions or no actions, we choose an action among those that pre-exist. Thus a person is an alienated being, who has a source of his or her own and is never affected by outside reality.

In the cover page of his *Being and Time*, Heidegger writes with respect to *Dasein* (Being) that: "Our aim is to work out the question of the meaning of Being and to do so concretely. Our provisional aim is the interpretation of time as the possible horizon for any understanding whatsoever of being."[48] Later in chapter three of the book under the sub-heading "Dasein's Authentic Potentiality-for-Being-a-Whole, and, Temporality as the Ontological Meaning of Care" he claims:

> Inasmuch as Dasein understands itself in a way which, proximally and for the most part, is inauthentic, we may suppose that 'time' as ordinarily understood does indeed represent a genuine phenomenon, but one which is derivative [ein abkünftiges]. It arises from inauthentic temporality, which has a source of its own.[49]

But for Kierkegaard, the interpretation of time as the possible horizon under which being is to be determined, as is also the case in Kant, directly opposes human experience. As Wyschogrod promptly points out: "Ontologically understood, it is not the presence of freedom that gives being to the possibilities in the situation. The possibilities that can be chosen pre-exist; all freedom does is to choose one or another of them."[50] According to Kierkegaard, freedom does not imply creating possibilities in a situation; rather possibilities are created or given to us. The origin of those possibilities is the transcendent, which is the absolute condition of being. How he derives that conclusion is by virtue of subjectivity. He astutely declares in his *Concluding Unscientific Postscript to the Fragments*, "an objective uncertainty held fast in an appropriation process of the most passionate inwardness is truth."[51] Hence the question of truth essentially is never about its objectivity. That is because God is not an object of historical or rational proof.

That does not mean God is not an object of our experience. The truth is our experience of God results from a subjective relation. The relation is about how one inwardly relates to the truth proclaimed in Christianity which purports to the idea of natural experience of the transcendent.[52] For Kierkegaard, the question of God is frequently raised in consequence of life experience of moral limitations/inadequacy and perplexity (i.e., anxiety, dread, fear, hope and so on). In other words, God is sought at our deepest level.

And just as he treats the problem of truth subjectively, he views freedom in the same way. A being is not alienated from the world as, for instance, Heidegger and others claim. We never cease to relate to the outside reality, in perceiving the world as constructs of the transcendent. Freedom is part of that construct.

Apparently Kierkegaard sees freedom from beyond temporality. Not only does he propose God as the origin of freedom, but that our choices are divinely necessitated. They are not implicitly necessary choices, but point to God's eternal purpose. Every choice entails God's dominant act of persuasion on humanity.

Freedom in Interdependence with the Divine

Unlike Heidegger, and Kant for that matter, who severs the self from God and the world, Kierkegaard puts freedom in dialectical relation to the transcendent. In that regard there are a few things to note. First, as we already noted, Kierkegaard affirms an intersecting boundary between God and humanity. That intersection is the point at which God is historically encountered and sought. Here I find theologian Paul Tillich to be helpful.

Tillich justly links Kierkegaard to having championed the cause for human freedom. In his *Systematic Theology* Tillich gives an analysis of human freedom in Kierkegaard by touching on an important concept which is at the core of his (Kierkegaard) philosophical anthropology: infinite passion. This is what he writes:

> If the word 'existential' points to a participation which transcends both subjectivity and objectivity, then man's relation to the gods is rightly called 'existential.' Man cannot speak of the gods in detachment. The moment he tries to do so, he has lost the god and has established just one more object within the world of many objects. Man can speak of the gods only on the basis of his relation to them. This relation oscillates between the concreteness of give-and-take attitude, in which the divine beings easily become objects and tools for human purposes, and the absoluteness of a total surrender on the side of man. The absolute element of man's ultimate concern demands absolute intensity, infinite passion (Kierkegaard), in the religious relation. The concrete element derives men toward an unlimited amount of relative action and emotion in the cult in which the ultimate concern is embodied and actualized, and also outside it.[53]

Tillich's firsthand analysis of a Kierkegaardian concept of freedom is proven to be plausible. That is the case in the sense Kierkegaardian subjectivity is filled with infinite passion (for the eternal) which logically implies our actual (transcendental) freedom (ft).

The self's infinite passion is a correlate of the transcendent. Passion toward the transcendent entails God's relation with the world. It denotes a concrete situation of our metaphysical or religious existence. Eternal passion, which Tillich calls "holiness," is an "experienced phenomenon." It is "open to phenomenological description." Thus the concept of infinite passion "is an important doorway to understanding the divine."

> The holy and the divine must be interpreted correlatively. A doctrine of God which does not include the category of holiness is not only unholy but also untrue. Such a doctrine transforms the gods into secular objects whose existence is rightly denied by naturalism. On the other hand, a doctrine of the holy which does not interpret it as the sphere of the divine transforms the holy into something aesthetic-emotional, which is the danger of theologies like those of Schleiermacher and Rudolf Otto. Both mistakes can be avoided in a doctrine of God which analyzes the meaning of ultimate concern and which derives from it both the meaning of God and the meaning of the holy.[54]

Because passion denotes freedom in Kierkegaard, Tillich's primary concern with passion or holiness as such is depicted via his ontological analysis of the ways in which human freedom is experienced. Below is his contribution.

According to Tillich, passion or freedom—in its religious feature—can be experienced in three different ways: "deliberation," "decision" and "responsibility." First, deliberation means "an act of weighing (*librare*) arguments and motives." According to Tillich, "The person who does the weighing is above the motives." That is, "as long as he weighs them, he is not identical with any of the motives but is free from all of them."[55]

Second, the term decision conveys the idea of cutting. In German language, the word *Ent-Schidung*, the image of *scheiden*, is in view here which means "to separate."[56] A decision, he says, "cuts off possibilities." It depicts the meaning that in a person's each decision a number of other possibilities are cut off or "excluded."[57]

Third, the term responsibility points to an obligation to respond in freedom to questions regarding one's decisions. In further denoting its meaning Tillich writes:

> He [a person] cannot ask anyone else to answer for him. He alone must respond, for his acts are determined neither by something outside him nor by any part of him but by the centered totality of his being. Each of us is responsible for what has happened through the center of his self, the seat and organ of his freedom.[58]

Tillich's account of freedom in Kierkegaard does not detract from Kierkegaard's own concept. For the most part, Kierkegaard would accept Tillich's account of human freedom as acts of deliberation, decision and responsibility. For Kierkegaard, too, places freedom in the existential sphere of momentous becoming where the subject is constantly faced with the challenge of making choices.

Yet, those choices are not in disjunction with the divine but made within the broader reality of the infinite. Hence we may call the God-human relation in Kierkegaard a form of synergy. A Kierkegaard scholar, Jamie Ferreira, affirms that view. She does it by stating freedom always manifests as "an interested, contextualized freedom" in Kierkegaard. That is, freedom as an existential aspect of human life is always interconnected with an outside being.

Kierkegaard, she says, distinguishes between true freedom and freedom of choice. According to Ferreira, Kierkegaard holds true freedom is compatible with there being no choice. A true freedom sets itself apart from freedom of choice or free will. In the words of Paul Tillich, "A *thing* as a completely determined object lacks freedom." That is because: "The *freedom* of a *thing* is a contradiction in terms."[59]

What Ferreira is pointing to is freedom's dialectical concept. It succumbs to both ideal and objective experience. As Tillich, for instance, poignantly notes a thing "lacks freedom." And freedom is not a thing (determined object). It transcends an object of determined quality in its indeterminable character. Therefore, "the freedom of a thing" (i.e., the will) is a contradiction in terms."[60] Such is the way in which, then, Kierkegaard's concept of freedom has to be taken.

Revelation, Authority, and the Case of Adler

Earlier we noted the concept of leap—a qualitative transition from the historical to the eternal. We had said it involves God as the constraining factor in the choice. That transition—from the historical to the eternal—is not solely human-willed. In Kierkegaard, the transition is preceded by a pre-given condition of faith. Hence, the leap occurs at the critical verge which is created between what precedes the ascent, namely the knowledge of and belief in the transcendent.

At this point we may safely conclude all of Kierkegaard's concepts of human life point to the fact that he is a religious thinker. He delineates all of his concepts from the Bible, including his view on human freedom and its relation to the transcendent, who is the author of our freedom.

Anyone who reads Kierkegaard's work easily sees how he uses the Bible as a literary device in his writings. That is important to note since it is something which is commonly overlooked. He applies the Bible to giving interpretations in all of his writings. He does that, not just to demonstrate the obvious fact of his religious identity as a Christian thinker, but also in engaging with troubling issues of his time using the text as the solution.

According to Kierkegaard scholar Jolita Pons (who favors the above view), the Bible and revelation are the ultimate basis for the truth in Kierkegaard.[61] According to another scholar, L. Joseph Rosas, Kierkegaard worked from and assumed the truths of biblical material precisely in order to resolve the problem of the paradox in human life.[62]

A book which clearly presents his serious appeal to the Bible is *The Book on Adler*. There, Kierkegaard gives an account of a minister who has lost his reason and experiences ambiguity of concepts. The intent is to reveal the frivolity of religious thinking of his day by showing how people (so called Christians) no longer believed in revelation and deviated from the truth. To his own question, "Why expose Adler?" he answers Adler is insane, and declares insanity is common among ecclesial leaders.

The insanity which Kierkegaard points to with respect to Adler comes from a "real spiritual movement toward inner self-concern."[63] Adler makes a claim that he has received revelation from God. That claim leads to suspension and removal from his pastoral post after giving inconsistent replies to a church's ecclesial inquisitions.[64] One may easily observe Adler as attempting to circumvent the authority of the church. But Kierkegaard projects a different view.

According to him, the book is "essentially about the confusion from which the concept of revelation (the bible, Incarnation and so on) suffers in his age; or about the fact that the concept of authority has been entirely forgotten in his confused age" by individuals and institutions.[65]

Adler is a prime example of one who suffers from that confusion. Adler is charged with taking what is normally a religious discourse between a believer and the deity as a revelation and using that as part of an attempt to circumvent the authority of the church, which dominates the culture. The condition poses great danger of obstructing the very core of the Christian faith by both Adler and the church, namely God's revelation and authority.

The problem of deifying the encounter with the deity is not just restricted to Adler's case. It includes the whole religious community, namely it testifies to the forgotten divine authority which he tries to restore. A Kierkegaard scholar, Norman Lilligard, acutely observes in his essay, "Revelation, Interpretation, Authority," that the theme in Kierkegaard's *Book on Adler* concerns the problem of authority. He points out: "The concepts of revelation and interpretation are treated in that work as functions of the concept of authority."[66] That is the primary issue in the book. It is about the problem of culture's (church and society) disobedience.

According to Lilligard, the problem which Kierkegaard has with Adler, and with his culture, is the confusion about the meaning of divine authority and revelation with human authority. The cause is an ambiguous distinction (forgetfulness) between the absolute (God, eternal) and the relative (historical, human).

> 'The calamity of the age,' Kierkegaard claimed, is 'not doubt about the truth of the religious but insubordination to the authority of the religious.' This calamity is partly the result of conceptual malaise. The concept of authority, Kierkegaard avers, has 'been entirely forgotten' in his age. In his view the forgetfulness is not innocent. It is due to lack of character and to insubordination. The kind of conceptual clarity that is required is a mark of moral respect for qualitative distinctions. The age, and Adler, lack that respect, he claims.[67]

In defining what he calls "forgetfulness" (of authority) in Kierkegaard, Lilligard states:

> Forgetfulness is part of a general 'leveling process' that includes as a crucial component the invasion of the ethical/religious domain by 'disinterested knowing.' By it he means the 'offense' that occurs in the situation of contemporaneity is avoided. Readers familiar with Kierkegaard's other writings, particularly the *Philosophical Fragments*, will understand how central the concept of contemporaneity becomes for him. And of course 'disinterested knowing,' particularly the speculative sort popular in his own Hegelianized age, is the butt of jokes and the target of his polemic throughout his writings."[68]

A few things concerning Lillegard's account above are in order. First, Lillegard correctly alludes to the fact that the problem of Adler and the age concerns their denial or disinterestedness in knowing the revelation. Second, the problem of denial is deeply rooted in disobedience or the polemical nature of the human spirit.

With respect to the first (problem of denial), in seeing his culture as religiously and morally impoverished he depicts the cause to be "self-deification." With respect to the second (problem of disobedience), Kierkegaard saw the problem had a spiritual root, namely human sin.

Seeing the problem of authority as primary focus of *The Book on Adler*, Lilligard notes Kierkegaard views revelation as "coming to individuals, apostles, and prophets, who are then able to speak with authority."[69]

> What needs to be emphasized is that even though the occasion of this book was a Danish pastor's claim that Jesus spoke to him, there is no discussion of content of what Jesus has said. Furthermore, Adler, at the inquisition, denies the truth of the event.[70]

According to Lilligard, "it is quite clear that what the *Book on Adler* is concerned with is divine discourse which should be distinguished from revelation." "The attempt," he says, "to treat discourse as revelation easily assimilates to a kind of romanticism in which the normativity of discourse disappears." That, he says, is what Kierkegaard sought to avoid.

In the *Book on Adler*, Kierkegaard's commitment to uphold God's revelation in distinction from all else is clear. And when in characterizing the disturbed age he often repeats and claims his role as one who is to provide the correct remedies. For instance, he describes it as absent-minded and calls for presence of mind; he finds them light-minded and calls for earnestness and sobriety. He finds his age distraught and feels called to provide attention.[71]

Kierkegaard tells us in the preface of the book he uses Adler's case "to defend dogmatic concepts" (divine revelation and authority). By that he does not mean giving a narrow and compressed dogmatic defense. Instead he backs them as being dogmatic or deductive, transporting their own biblical content which he says theology (under the great curse of Hegelian-speculative thought) in his time failed to do.[72] Hence, those who ignore the Bible as God's revelation in Kierkegaard's works will overlook many subtleties of meaning that originate from the reliance on the Scripture.

Unfortunately many readers miss that crucial biblical dimension in his thought. As Pons sadly states, "Kierkegaard scholarship has suffered from underestimating the role of the bible in his so called philosophical or aesthetical writings."

A case in point: in the past some thinkers approached Kierkegaard from a purely philosophical point of view without even a rudimentary knowledge of the bible, and extracted his concepts for their philosophical purpose. For instance, Husserl, Heidegger, Sartre and others extracted concepts such as anxiety, dread and existence as fitting themes for philosophical meditation, pulling the Kierkegaardian oeuvre into a different direction.[73] Below is a particular case of Sartre's appropriation.

Sartre's Appropriation of Kierkegaard

Among others, French philosopher Jean Paul Sartre is notoriously known for appropriating Kierkegaard's works for his philosophical purpose. As a case in point, we first refer to William McBride's work "Sartre's Debts to Kierkegaard: A Partial Reckoning." There McBride notes: "the influence of Kierkegaard on Sartre's earlier formation, and hence on existentialism as a whole, was capital is a commonplace."[74] He adds:

> Rare is the level of appreciation that Sartre conveys for an individual with whose thought he is, on the surface, in such profound disagreement—and in fact in disagreement on the very issue that, for Kierkegaard, ultimately meant everything, the issue of Christian faith.[75]

McBride rightly points out Kierkegaard had great influence on Sartre's thinking. He argues Kierkegaard's philosophy played a major role in shaping Sartre's overall philosophical outlook on the world. The problem is "Sartre appropriates Kierkegaard for [his] purposes."[76] He extracts Kierkegaard's concept of being and freedom applies to constructing his own concept. But what is absent in his system is that which essentially underlies Kierkegaard's works, namely Christian faith.

Nonetheless, Sartre's analysis of the human self ironically helps us to better understand Kierkegaard's concept of subjectivity or freedom. Like Kierkegaard, Sartre analyzes the relation between the self and the world. He too, as does Kierkegaard, builds that relation "by taking up a point of view from which its environment is structured."[77] The problem, however, lies in the concept of the self as a self-relation in Kierkegaard taking a form of gap between the self and its actions in Sartre.

Touching on this important matter, Sartre scholar Manuela Hackel insists:

> At first glance, one cannot see the affinity to Kierkegaard's concept of nothingness. However, Sartre's explanation of why consciousness is able to negate, establishes the connection. Consciousness, that is, freedom—Sartre localizes freedom in the

[spontaneity of consciousness]—is its own nothingness. What Kierkegaard describes as the leap—the impossibility of explaining free action—returns in Sartre as 'a discontinuity between the motives and the act'"[78]

Manuela correctly sees in Sartre: "The human being always realizes himself at a distance: the objects of the world, to himself, to his own past and future."[79]

But in affirming human freedom Sartre disconnects himself from the religious context of Kierkegaard's thought. Contrary to Kierkegaard, he dissociates himself from the transcendent. He sees the self as the source of all objectivities. The source of transcendence is the self. Unlike Kierkegaard who directs the cause and aim of existence to the transcendent—God, Sartre notes the essential aim in life is to give descriptions of the self in disconnection with anything other.

Despite Kierkegaard's great influence, Sartre shows no religious tone in his theoretical conveyance.

> Sartre came increasingly to concentrate—under the influence of Soren Kierkegaard—on the problem of understanding human beings in concrete life-situations. Sartre's focus thus came to be the idea of radical human freedom, which he regarded as condemnation and opportunity at the same time. Radical human freedom is condemnation because the single individual is completely helpless in the face of his decisions, which [give birth to themselves autonomously], but nevertheless [has to accept responsibility without being able to justify himself]. Yet it is also opportunity inasmuch as the individual's life is open for self-creation, independently of moral or social bondage.[80]

Sartre's theory of the self, we may say, clarifies Kierkegaard's position on the problem of existence as what Hackel calls "facticity [existence or being] and transcendence [eternal passion]." His detailed description of subjectivity—as reality and non-reality—most closely represents the structure of Kierkegaard's dialectical view on subjectivity as both historical and eternal.

Interestingly, Hackel raises an important fact that Sartre considers transcendence later in life as an exteriority. He contends Sartre comes to believe the self implies an inescapable effect of the transcendent as the ground of being. Sartre draws a conclusion: "No situation is ever determined; the individual always has a choice." He adds: "The self always keeps distance to what is given. Its ability to transcend the facts makes it possible for him to overcome constraints and to find alternative actions."[81]

But, Sartre's transcendence or transcendent is far too different from the one conceived by Kierkegaard. Whereas the transcendent conveys religious tone in Kierkegaard, Sartre's concept is humanistic.[82]

This is made apparent in his book *Being and Nothingness*. There Sartre refers to his philosophy as a "phenomenological ontology." Unlike metaphysics, phenomenological ontology attempts to describe being apart from principles. Metaphysics as we know it is concerned with the question as to why there is something rather than nothing. It seeks to discover the first principle of being. Sartre's interest however is in giving basic descriptions of existence and not its origin.[83]

He tends to bypass the all too familiar opposition between idealism and realism for a definite kind of relationship between consciousness and the world which is grounded in the self. The self is the source of objectivities. Its meaning is found in the world apart from an ideal.

His ontology of existence reflects an uncanny character of presenting the methodological understanding of the self as steeped in one's inner self. As one scholar, Marjorie Grene, observes: "The Sartrean individual is utterly alone, wholly responsible, making himself as the negation of a barren field of being, it itself wholly devoid of meaning, or even, in its inertia, of power."[84] The self is its own being, devoid of meaning, caught between being and nothingness where the latter is its essential ground.

> The for-itself in its being is failure because it is the foundation only of itself as nothingness. In truth this failure is its very being [?], but it has meaning only if the for-itself apprehends itself as failure in the presence of the being which it has failed to be; that is, of the being which would be the foundation of its being and no longer merely the foundation of its nothingness—or, to put it another way, which would be its foundation as coincidence with itself…Human reality is its own surpassing toward what it lacks; it surpasses itself towards the particular being which it would be if it were what it is.[85]

Therefore, one exists before his or her unreflective consciousness. Consciousness is a particular object. It is no spirit and no reflection. To be aware is fundamentally to be or engaged in a dialectical relation with the self.

Hence in spite of the being dialectical thinkers, Kierkegaard and Sartre differ when it comes to factoring in transcendence as a necessary experience. With respect to Sartre:

> Even as dialecticians the two writers [Kierkegaard and Sartre] differ, at least in the overall direction of their respective dialectics. Granted, they both are Hegelian, and

as such their philosophical interests and arguments are similar, often strikingly so. Thus Sartre's use of modal concepts [i.e., look, shame and others] in Being and Nothingness, for example, is reminiscent of Kierkegaard on possibility and necessity in the Bits.[86]

He goes on to say:

Sartre's account of the immediate structures of the for-itself, again, strikingly resembles Kierkegaard's account of the self in The Sickness to Death. Thus Kierkegaard, in a passage which is both a parody of Hegelian method and its apotheosis: 'The self is a relation which relates itself to its own self, or it is that in the relation the relation relates to its own self.' Sartre similarly detaches the self from substantial status, and makes it, though more negatively, relational: 'The for-itself is the being which determines itself to exist in as much as it cannot coincide with itself.'[87]

Kierkegaard's concept of consciousness on the other hand is in close association with the eternal.[88] Freedom compels transcendental reflection of the divine. Freedom is an essential being/reality of human essence integrated into an experience of the transcendent. Freedom does not imply autonomy. It is not independently self-governing as is the case with humanist thinkers such as Sartre and others (i.e., Kant, Nietzsche, Husserl, Heidegger and so on).

Freedom is meaningless outside the experience of the transcendent. The reason is it fails to provide the interpretation for the mediating self. As Kant for instance points out, unless we posit certain universal and necessary principles in human existence we have no way of inquiring about human cognition, thus human existence; because the question regarding existence ultimately arrives at asking about the transcendental or ideal deduction of the self which cannot derive from a purely empirical deduction.

There are two reasons for this: first, the transcendental or ideal deduction of the self for Kant, and Kierkegaard, comes from metaphysics; second, the deduction is genuine in showing its necessity.

In that deduction being is revealed as positive (being) and negative (non-being). In both cases the self is depicted of its temporal nature. They constitute the essential structure of our being. In describing Sartre's structural concept of being Grene states:

Sartre, good Cartesian as he is, begins with consciousness, the for-itself, but is directed by Husserl to its target, which, in Hegelian fashion, he describes as sheer being, as the in-itself. The for-itself-in-itself is then what his for-itself is in search of. Being in the mode of what is other than being, it longs to be simply, or rather to be what it is—that is, to be for-itself and so not to be simply, and yet to be for-itself as being is, as being pure and simple.[89]

If such is the case, which I believe is, then Sartre's concept of the self apparently takes a Hegelian form. But, by beginning the analysis of the self with reflection his conclusion is much more pessimistic. He is more concerned with the question of being as for-itself than he is with the in-itself.

> The concepts he (Sartre) is working with have also already been exhibiting their characteristically Hegelian stamp. The overall movement of Hegelian dialectic is from mere being, in-itself, through consciousness, for-itself, to what Hegel considers the ultimate ground of all reality—the Concept as Being-in-and-for-itself.[90]

Sartre is definitely concerned with discovering the essential makeup of the human self. Whereas some (i.e., Heidegger and others) define being as the framework of philosophical reflection on being, Sartre uses nothingness as a way to gain the meaning of being.

> Sartre uses Nothingness to open up Being: it is nihilation that makes the for-itself the being it is—namely, the being that has to be what It is not and not be what it is. Instead of digging down into Dasein, as Heidegger does to uncover the temporality on which it has always already rested, a temporality which had been half seen in the inadequate understanding of Being characteristic of the human manner of being in the world.[91]

In the words of Grene, for Sartre "Being and Nothingness are the dialectical contraries par excellence."[92] And yet, those contraries fundamentally structure the essence of being. However, the difference between Sartre and Kierkegaard is that Kierkegaard makes necessary reference to the transcendent whereas Sartre dismisses it.

Theologians are not exceptions to this stifling. According to Pons: "It is even more surprising that despite many theological interpretations of Kierkegaard's works that only a few theologians have looked at how he actually uses the bible in his texts."[93] That does not mean only those who have thorough knowledge of the bible can approach Kierkegaard's texts. On the contrary, Kierkegaard holds that even those who approach his texts without the slightest knowledge of the bible will gain knowledge of the bible.

Kierkegaard's works are not primarily about the bible. But it serves as the foundation of his writings. His works reveal clear presence of the bible and suggest that the possibility of relating to God for his age or otherwise is only through becoming interested in the Word and properly internalizing it. According to Pons, the *imitatio Christi* begins with none other than the imitation of Christ's Word and the concepts, such as imitation, contemporaneity and appropriation to which Kierkegaard apportions meanings of great significance in his writings all have an intimate relation to the bible as their source.[94]

For that reason, Kierkegaard is often called a theologian in spite of his renowned (but often misinterpreted) poetic and psychological [and philosophical] temperament.[95] Kierkegaard scholar Arnold Come is in rapport with that view. According to Come:

> It must be noted that when Kierkegaard says he is a poet, he almost always adds "and thinker" (Taenker). This term is equivalent for "theologian." Just as he writes "discourses" and not "sermons" because he is "without authority" of ordination, so he uses "thinker" to indicate that he is theologian but not appointed.[96]

Pons argues once Kierkegaard is taken as a theologian everything fits into and become subject to this presupposition.[97]

For sure, the bible and revelation have an important place in Kierkegaard's works. The more we read of his works the more we discover their apparent relation to the bible. Whether one reads *Philosophical Fragments* and *Training in Christianity* for a religious discourse or *The Concept of Dread* and *The Concept of Anxiety* for existential and psychological reflection, it is clear that the corpus of his works is essentially and profoundly rooted in his biblical views. Hence, they deserve a careful attention to all the nuances that are contained in them.

Faith, God and Freedom

Not surprisingly, then, Kierkegaard draws the meaning of God-freedom relation from the bible. What he discovers is one does not make a choice in sheer arbitrariness. He states God is always imposed on our decisions. And unlike the view of Timothy Jackson and others who see Kierkegaard as conveying a Pelagian view of the autonomy of the will, we instead find a strongly biblical element in Kierkegaard's concept, namely grace. This is because Kierkegaard holds human reason collides with the transcendent. Human will or freedom does not hold the possibility of the leap. It is restrained by its finitude.

In that collision two things occur. First, the Socratic imagination of the truth is completely shattered; the notion of recollection becomes incredible.

Second, a different approach to the paradox emerges. One assumes the paradox to be accessible by something equally supernatural, namely faith.

At this point an awareness of the paradox in its dual distinction of the absolute and the historical sets in. As one scholar correctly advocates, God's Incarnation in the world as "the polemical Christology (of God in history)" separates itself "from literally all other approaches: from the religious and societal approaches of contemporary 'Christendom,' as well as from the intellectual trends of historical or speculative academic theology."[98]

For example, Kierkegaard's bifurcation of the eternal and the historical in the Incarnation restricts our intelligibility to having true representation of the event. That restriction points to a different solution for the Incarnation: faith or grace. Without debunking the congruency between faith and reason/freedom, he acknowledges both in order to do justice to the teachings of the bible, which acknowledges God's absoluteness and human freedom simultaneously.[99]

What he sees in that God-freedom relation is "the interpenetration of the rhythms of *diastasis* and *synthesis*." According to Kierkegaard scholar Paul Sponheim, Kierkegaard encounters in the God-freedom relation the interpenetration of the rhythms of the divine and the human in which each strand preserves its identity without suffering the objectivity of the other. He contends Kierkegaard does not find a discernible trait in the relation.

According to Sponheim, Kierkegaard does not see any discernible result delineating from that relation. If anything is unique, it is the fact that the relation is rationally indiscernible. Even though one is an agent of his or her own actions, those actions are transcendently interposed. All our historical occurrences are achieved on both sides of the horizon, the historical and the eternal.

This unity of the eternal and the historical—without disparaging their identity of a priori synthesis—gives a solution to the God-freedom problem. It simultaneously affirms the truth of God's absolute intervention and the passive role of human task in making choices. Unlike Kant's critique, which posits the self-originating causality of the will in the subject, Kierkegaard offers the solution of reconciliation and overthrows philosophy's assumption of freedom's independence.

For that reason, Kierkegaard is critical of Hegelian idealism. In it, he says, existence is lost or forgotten in reflection. In *The Present Age*, Kierkegaard writes: "Our age is essentially one of understanding and reflection."[100] Here, he alludes to his current philosophical trend, Hegelian philosophy, sweeping through Denmark bearing great impact on theologians and philosophers. Just what is Hegelian philosophy and why was Kierkegaard so critical of it? In the next section, we will try to give answers.

Hegel and Kierkegaard on Freedom

Many thinkers, before and after Kant, thought knowledge was to be understood differently, namely metaphysically, from how it once was thought. They defined it in terms of something obtained through science. However, the scientific way of knowing is only one of many which are open to knowledge.

Others include perception, intuition, understanding and concepts, all of which can also be called knowledge.[101] It is important to see that in later years the realists and pragmatists have overlooked the important fact that scientific knowledge is only a fraction in the comte cache of different sorts and ignored the reliable claims of unscientific ones.

In elaborating on this problem, German philosopher Richard Kroner states in his *Culture and Faith* that natural scientists cannot help relying on unscientific principles for their scientific knowledge. For scientific knowledge always stands on unscientific pre-assumptions. Kroner correctly argues: "Like all of us, he [scientist] depends upon immediate experience of the surrounding world, of the persons with whom he lives, of the circumstances under which he lives, of the nation to which he belongs, of his country, and so on."[102] The rationale behind his assertion is that experience requires an unscientific or ideal explanation.

Modern philosophers, according to Kroner, picked out sense-experience as the original type of all experience of knowledge. They almost exclusively examined our relation to nature and the experience of the world.[103] The total importance of one's experience of being and the world takes its prime effect and is highly admired in the romantic era in Europe, in which Hegel first calls attention to its broad scope and important meaning. He does it not only for the purpose of scientific inquiry but for the inquiry into all spheres of human experience.[104]

In *The Phenomenology of Mind*, Hegel takes us through the world of experience beyond the scope of reason in order to arrive at an ultimate reality. In the words of philosopher Walter Kaufmann, the book "takes the reader through all the worlds of experience, personal and impersonal, individual and generic, intellectual and emotional, moral and political, aesthetic and religious" until, in the end, he concludes with the knowledge which brings all other knowl-edge from the previous stages: "Absolute Knowledge."[105]

Hegel relates his book as "The Science of the Experience of Conscious-ness." It means what consciousness experiences in all of the stages of his-torical development is the consciousness itself. Not realizing its aim at first, consciousness, in unity with the Spirit, goes through all of the stages as such in order to realize its absoluteness.[106] Religion is one of those stages. Religion, says Hegel, is part of that unified whole.

But according to Kierkegaard, Hegel's concept of religion is problematic. It is so for two reasons. First, it raises a metaphysical problem. It pretentiously claims to have the truth. Second, it raises an existential problem. Hegel's con-cept of truth excludes the self in the Spirit's historical flow towards its final objectivity: absolute knowing.

Here, I find Kierkegaard scholar Jon Stewart to be helpful. According to Stewart, Kierkegaard's primary concern with Hegel's absolute idealism can be found in *Philosophical Fragments*. Stewart notes: "the danger, which [Johannes] Climacus points out, is that speculative philosophy can distract and seduce one into thinking in an exclusively objective manner so that the fundamen-tal question about one's own eternal happiness is never raised."[107] Stewart conveys that is precisely the concern which is demonstrated in the *Postscript*. There Climacus writes:

> For the speculative thinker the question of his personal eternal happiness cannot come up at all, precisely because his task consists in going away from himself more and more and becoming objective and in that way disappearing from himself and becoming the gazing power of speculative thought.[108]

The danger which Kierkegaard perceives in speculative philosophy, Hege-lian or otherwise, it abstracts humanity in its attempt to set the world-reality from the viewpoint of absolute consciousness. As Stewart argues:

> Speculative thought tends to abstract from the individual since it aims at an analysis of the whole. Thus, the danger for a potential Christian believer is that one could forget oneself entirely in the abstraction of speculative thought and thus forget the issue of one's eternal happiness.[109]

According to Kierkegaard, if one follows Hegel he or she arrives at abstracting God and reality.[110] There are two reasons for that. First, Hegelian knowledge is mediated. Second, Hegel does not permit religion to be brought in from outside. The so called religion is to be "mechanically produced and placed within being.[111] He sees the world in all of its particulars "by means of thought which *passes through and encompasses* them."[112] It is not a "theory next to the practical," as it were. Instead, it is an "activity which moves through both theory and practice."[113]

Kierkegaard reveals Hegel's misguided view of the world which disparages God and humanity.[114] His analysis of the transcendent outside metaphysics does not end up being "anything more than approximation." "And there is an essential misrelation between that and a personal, infinite interestedness in one's own eternal happiness."[115] In general, "Nothing pertaining to faith results from critical theological scholarship."[116] Just as we saw in Kant, reason takes the supremacy over and against religion as the origin of historical objectivities in Hegel.

In his *Fear and Trembling*, Kierkegaard shows a different stance on the God-world relation. He declares: "personal existence, in 'moving beyond [*depassant*]' the aesthetic stage, also 'transcends [*depasse*]' ethics in order to enter the religious realm of a faith that no longer lets itself be justified on external [rational] grounds."[117] That means, for instance, the God-world relation in Kierkegaard is not a conceptual assembly constructed in a circular flow of scientific progress as in Hegel.[118] According to Hegel:

> What is essential for science is not so much that something purely immediate should constitute the beginning but rather that the whole of it is a circle in which the first also becomes that last, and the last also the first. The line of scientific progress thus becomes a circle.[119]

Neither the transcendent object (Absolute Spirit) nor immanent subject (humanity) is concretely present in Hegel. One is the other and the other is the other. As one critic notes:

> For Hegel, the developing world of nature and finite spirit is an unfolding of Absolute Spirit itself. Put crudely, the world is not made out of nothing. It is formed out of God's own substance in a process of self-expression. There is a sense in which, for Hegel and Hegelians, God and the world are one reality, and not two.[120]

Hegel's concept forms an unlawful unity between God and the world. With respect to the transcendent the eternal object is radically humanized. And humanity is disparaged of its being. It debunks one's relevancy and existential significance. Essentially, the concept contradicts the theological heritage of biblical authority. Biblical authority and revelation do not play the central role in his system.

Absence of biblical foundation in Hegel and how he supplants the supernatural claims of Christianity with development of human morality is not a petty issue for Kierkegaard. The problem requires having a clear perspective from the religious standpoint. Hegel's God is not the God revealed in the Bible. His God is equal with the world. Hence Kierkegaard's charge:

> If Hegel had written the whole of his logic and then said, in the preface, that it was merely an experiment in thought in which he had even begged the question in many places, then he would certainly have been the greatest thinker who had ever lived. As it is he is merely comic.[121]

A critic, William Desmond, points out what Hegel intends is to self-transcend and unite with the transcendent. However, the result is a failure. The subject forgets, perhaps deliberately, the qualitative gap between God and the self thus transforming the transcendent into an immanent being.

> We find an erotic absolute [in Hegel]. An erotic absolute is one modeled on a certain understanding of self-transcending being. One that surpasses an initial indefiniteness, that others itself, determines itself as other to its initial indefiniteness, but comes to itself again more fully, by relating explicitly to itself in that otherness.[122]

Hegel's concept, hence, is a fatuous comedy. It is an irreverent scheme of thought's erotic opening to the transcendent beyond its limits. It cleverly transforms the God-world relation into a scientific scheme and objectifies them as a single reality. It is an invention: the concept falsely unites God and the world.[123]

According to theologian Hans Küng, "Hegel understands the reality of the one who is Son of God and Son of man, i.e. of the God-man, in terms of the unity of the totality of life. It is *for this reason* that he is concerned with a 'holy mystery.'" He goes on to say: "it is also *for this reason* that he [Hegel] is concerned with 'faith' in contrast to the knowledge of the reflective intellect." According to Küng:

> Intellectual knowledge of a reflective and therefore also of a disruptive and destructive kind cannot grasp this relationship between Jesus the Son of God and the Father. With an eye to the two natures doctrines of traditional Christology, which united two substances by way of reflective thought, Hegel states that '[K]nowledge posits, for its way of taking this relation, two natures of different kinds, a human nature and a divine one, a human essence and a divine one, each with personality and substantiality and, whatever their relation, both remaining two because they are posited as absolutely different.[124]

He goes on to say:

> This starting-point puts us on the horns of a dilemma between unity and difference
> from which there is no avenue of escape for the intellect: 'Those who posit this
> absolute difference and yet still require us to think of these absolutes as one in their
> inmost relationship do not dismiss the intellect on the ground that they are asserting
> a truth outside its scope. On the contrary, it is the intellect which they expect to
> grasp absolutely different substances which at the same time are an absolute unity.
> Thus they destroy the intellect in positing it. But whoever *denies* the unity of the
> natures thereby does away with Christ: Those who (i) accept the given difference
> of the substantialities but (ii) deny their unity are more logical. They are justified in
> (i), since it is required to think God and man, and therefore in (ii), since to cancel
> the cleavage between God and man would be contrary to the first admission they
> were required to make. In this way they save the intellect; but then they refuse to
> move beyond this absolute difference of essences, then they elevate the intellect,
> absolute division, destruction of life, to the pinnacle of spirit.[125]

For Küng and others, the main problem in Hegel is the convening of revelation historically. He fails to treat it as supernatural. For instance, Hegel does
not see the Incarnation as a transcendent event. He does not acknowledge
Christ as the divine in human form.

Here two things must be mentioned. First, in Hegel God's divine revelation is employed in such a way that the "dialectic of Trinitarian self-revelation
is speculatively interpreted as self-positing Subject and philosophically refor-
mulated as absolute reconciling Spirit."[126] Contrary to viewing Christ as "the
greatest possible, the infinite qualitative move from being God, and therefore
the profoundest cognition"—the great event which is inapprehensible to human thought but nonetheless actual—it is a mere phenomenal representation
of the immanent unity of God and the world soon to be realized in a worldly
form of an ideal paradigm which is far from being God's redemptive event in
the world.[127]

Second, Hegel's speculation from Kierkegaard's standpoint poses the
problem of freedom. Not only does Hegel transform the transcendent into
an abstract form and thus robs its eternal character, but he also abstracts humanity.[128]

In Hegel history appears before there is God-world unity. In Kierkegaard's
view history is a constituent part of but does not have precedence over existence, as Hegel erroneously thinks. For Kierkegaard, existence (freedom)
precedes history. History occurs in and through actions and interactions of
human subjects. Thus the organic movement of human spirit (Hegel) and

the like cannot be called history, a possibility of which Hegel posits in his system. Existence or freedom is what essentially unites the world with the transcendent. Hence, Hegel's depiction of existence fails to show historical possibilities are not enclosed in the circle of human subjectivity from Kierkegaard's point of view.

In his first journal entry, Kierkegaard shows his disassociation with the abstract concept of freedom and existence such as the one Hegel and Hegelians depict. In the next entry Kierkegaard goes as far as stating the next proceeding task was to concentrate one's thought on existence (freedom). After pointing out that an attempt was made in modern philosophy to outdo Kant's skepticism—by testing thought's ability as to how far it can grasp reality—and stating that Hegelian philosophy "arrived at the conclusion that earlier philosophy [of Kant] unreflectively assumed as a beginning that on the whole there is reality in thought" he asserts it now comes into what he calls "genuine anthropological 'contemplation'"[129] His other entries show this thought is immersed in deepening the focus on being.

In spite of his passionate criticism of Hegel, there are parts of his philosophy which we find obscure. For one, certain existential concepts such as dread, despair and others lack concrete meaning. Let's take the concept of despair for instance. Despair is an abstraction which cannot be definitely described. It has no concrete character.

But, there is a notable difference between Kierkegaard and Hegel. Whereas Hegel debunks all realities, Kierkegaard shows an inherent quality within those realities. In other words, Kierkegaardian concepts, unlike those of Hegel, depict real meaning.

For example, he calls despair a [real] "concern." It is a godly grief in relation to the transcendent though the concept remains mysteriously abstract.[130] That is because despair or any other existential concepts (i.e., dread, fear, anxiety and so on) are subjective. They are not a set of objective properties. Existence, he says, is all about the subjective. It is a "way" of being. Despair, he says, is what is experienced in the loss of the first state of innocence and doubts in sin whether a return to the original state of unity with God could be achieved. That uncertainty is a real concern occupying human life.

As the Hegelian system proposes an abstract unity of God and the world, Kierkegaard sees it as a deceptive move to unveil the truth (Absolute Spirit) in humanistic terms. He claims it is a dangerous concept which suggests correspondence between reality and the mind that disparages human existence and the transcendent. In Kant's language, God and history or humanity are not made sensible. Furthermore, the concept of that abstract unity between the two does not meet the requirement of being made sensible for the objective validity of its significance.[131]

The same Hegelian concept poses a greater problem regarding the paradox of the God-man. The problem is: "our theological understanding of the life and work of the person and work of Jesus of Nazareth."[132] For Kierkegaard God's revelation in Jesus is an impregnable, unacceptable, and impenetrable fact for the human understanding. It stands [alone] at the "un-crossable" border as that which "thought itself cannot think."[133] In its encounter:

> The human spirit is struck by the inexplicable fact of God's revelation; it encounters this fact, this phenomenon. It simply misunderstands it when it tries to approach this phenomenon of God's revelation and make it comprehensible in terms of historical science. God's revelation in Christ is an un-crossable boundary of our spirit, our reason; our science, our thought, but it is a boundary for us because it is absurd to our thought. That means it is something that can be proven impossible and thus certainly non-existent.[134]

The Incarnation cannot be pondered by human thought. The event does not demand rational consideration or solution. It shuts its doors to rational examination. It is a radical, inapprehensible and untouchable event. Yet, it is true. What it instead demands is belief. It demands synthesis of perception and assent or belief based on the ideal condition of transcendental reflection. Kierkegaard admits history or space is the condition of all experience, including the concept of the transcendent.

> This paradox does not permit any mediation; we cannot penetrate it intrinsically in any manner whatsoever. We can only declare and make comprehensible what we cannot understand, that it is incomprehensible. And what is peculiar is that we can say something about this absurdity because it is a "fact" [and is known as such]. It happened, when God's Son became man, and it is still happening in him today. Of such revealed fact, it must truly be evident that it does not offer our rational thought any single certainty or point of contact. The only certainty it supplies is the certainty that it does not offer any certainty, that we must reach the conclusion that it is objectively uncertain, yes, extremely improbable, yes, even impossible.[135]

Hence the event of Incarnation does not yield to logic. It cannot be apprehended. It is irrelevance and confusion, a sheer awe and curiosity, an intimidation and shame to our rationality. It stands paradigmatic from the standpoint of human reason. It is objective and paradoxical at the same time. It is void of being a single identity. But Hegel and other hybrids of modernity subject the event to modern reason which functions on logical categories. It does not have personal dimension.[136]

As Kant saw human beings as having statistical relations to some sociological prediction, Hegel and others thought it in terms of having abstract historical nature.[137] Rather than pointing to reason's limits as the event completely escapes the normative principle of the modern concept of humanity which evaded the subjective, modern philosophy exhibited pride in disparaging the occurrence. As John Wild correctly states:

> Modern philosophy has failed to come to grips with the human subject as lived from within. It has tried to deny it, to evade it, to detach it from the world. But nevertheless this subject exists. It cannot be denied and hangs over the whole succession of objective systems like a threatening cloud, breaking in at unexpected moments with shattering gusts of storm. It is inescapable, and yet unresponsive to all the prevailing modes of approach. In evading the 'subjective,' modern thought has been evading the act of existing, and this is no small evasion. To be right about everything but existence is very far from being right."[138]

The Incarnation, from the viewpoint of modern philosophy, remains a mere symbol. It is a symbolic unity of no historical or objective content.

The ultimate criticism deriving from the modern thought is Christ's undergoing humiliation and suffering in spite of his exalted nature. Truly impossible to be conceived by the lofty mind of modern thought, this ineffable *mysterium tremendum fascinas* remains an astonishment.

For Hegel and other modern thinkers, Christ is a "conceptual pre-figurement" which signifies teleological fulfillment of the Spirit's activity in the world. At the end, the world brings fulfillment of personal freedom. "Hegel's basic thought, as we have seen, was that world occurrence is a self-unfolding of the Spirit. The Spirit does not exist 'in-itself' over against the world. It gradually moves upward from the stage of unconscious nature to that of awakening consciousness [freedom] itself."[139]

For Hegel:

> Notion is also something that immediately is, and this distinction (of the in-itself and the for-itself) in so far as it is present in consciousness itself, is the determinate context, but since this content is at the same time a content grasped in thought, consciousness remains immediately aware of its unity with this determinate and distinct being, not, as in the picture thought, where consciousness still has specially to bear in mind that his is the picture thought; on the contrary, notion is for me straight away my notion. In thinking, I am free because I am not in another, but remain simply and solely in communion with myself, and the object which for me the essential being, is

undivided unity of my being-for-myself, and my activity in conceptual thinking is a movement within myself.[140]

Hegel's mediated unity, from a Christian or Kierkegaardian perspective, fits the description of a vast deceptive maneuver that is far from the biblical truth: The self is for itself.

What sets Kierkegaard apart from Hegel is his determinate interpretation of the self/freedom as having a real dimension. In Kierkegaard, freedom is thought's genuine category of something true. And it is held in balance between itself and the divine. For him, to acknowledge either freedom or God's omnipotence solely against the other is to be either fundamental (absoluteness of God) or liberal (absoluteness of freedom). Thus to hold the two in balance is a crucial task.

In doing so he preserves the difference and identity of the subject and the object. But the relation is one of tension wherein the divine limits the human. They do not exercise equal force. It connotes God's supremacy, his absoluteness over and against all historical objectivities. This way, Kierkegaard's formulation of the dialectic of opposites (God and humanity) demonstrates the root-structure of all of his subsequent rational concepts explored in his works, which is the supremacy of the Divine Creator over and against creation. As Lee Capel correctly states:

> it would appear that this correlation of opposites within the sphere of reflection is hyperbolically 'fastened together at the top' like pleasure and pain, like movement and repose, classicism and romanticism, identity and contradiction, and it is Kierkegaard's curious fusion of the two which makes the total structure and design of the essay an ironic whole—a singular gest.[141]

He concludes:

> Hegel's prescriptions for a classical work of art, the fact that his theory of 'substantial form' entails something like an isomorphism between inner and outer form, are applied to the romantic subject matter *par excellence*, namely, irony. The result is that although the conceptual significance of irony posits a formal *opposition* (the external is not the internal, the internal not the external—the essence is not the phenomenon, the phenomenon not the essence), and though this immanent form reduplicates itself in the medium of the work imparting to the linguistic expression its own shape (the pervasive Hegelianism of the essay conceals a discreet parody on Hegel, not to mention the Danish Hegelians); still, there remains an *identity* between the internal and the external though the formal assertion of the first be contradiction and the material enactment in the second contradictory, remains an organic unity between

essence and phenomenon though the implicit structure of the first be incommensurability and the explicit representation of the second exhibit itself as incommensurable.[142]

With respect to the difference between Hegel and Kierkegaard, Capel further explains:

> The classical harmony between the internal and the external, as formulated by Hegel, is here superimposed upon a romantic content whose inner and outer form is identical: contradiction. *Both* as essence *and* as phenomenon the internal is not the external, the external not the internal. The apparent similarity between Kierkegaard and Hegel is posited in real dissimilarity.[143]

As Capel correctly explains, the unity of those opposites is assigned different meanings in Kierkegaard and Hegel. Whereas Hegel assigns the sameness of the inner and outer structure of the reality, Kierkegaard assigns the distinction between the two. That is:

> For Hegel, irony is treated as a single moment in the development of the subjective or moral aspect of the ethical concept, all morality being regarded as the negation or further elaboration of a natural concrete ethic induced by the advent of reflection, a development wherein subjectivity ultimately seeks to isolate itself and hence degenerates into what Hegel terms 'the moral forms of evil' with irony (romantic assigned its place as the final phase in such an aberration, *the furthest reach of subjectivity*.[144]

Kierkegaard, on the other hand, gives a completely different understanding of irony in contrast to Hegelian concept. Irony, says Kierkegaard, is a moment in human subjectivity. It is the starting point of existence. The idea is indispensible and inseparable to human nature. "Kierkegaard regards irony as *the mere beginning of subjectivity*, and assigns to it the value of marking the birth of the personal life."[145]

According to Capel:

> He is concerned to give this reflective phenomenon an organic life of its own, and to induce irony to manifest itself and moment becomes for Kierkegaard a negative concept, a structured whole of experience in the medium of reflection which cannot be disposed of by a dialectical sleight of hand within the system but only experientially outlived in 'the dialectic of life' as it is inherently self-consuming. With only a semblance of fidelity to Hegel's dialectic, inasmuch as the definitions of the successive phases of the concept admit of dialectical formulae to combine in a quasi Hegelian 'deduction,' Kierkegaard plots three points which describe not a circle but a past, a life, a whole: the beginning, middle, and end of the career of irony—its inception

in the figure of Socrates, its illusory zenith in the romantics, and the point at which irony enigmatically disappears, experientially metamorphosed through resignation into self-mastery. The essential thing to notice, therefore, is how irony is overcome and what is able to overcome it: for Hegel the concrete universal, for Kierkegaard the concrete individual.[146]

Just as God takes the mastery over the irony of his relation with the world, the self takes the mastery over irony. Nonetheless irony is being's point of departure. That is made apparent in all his works.[147]

· 3 ·

UNITY OF FAITH AND REASON

Kierkegaard on Freedom and Grace

Despite the fact that Kierkegaard opposes human autonomy, some disagree. They argue he propagates autonomy and the fact is most transparent in his discussion of freedom and grace. One critic who advocates that argument is Timothy Jackson. Jackson states, "Kierkegaard and his pseudonyms offer a consistent, and consistently Arminian, account of grace and freedom."[1]

Jackson calls Kierkegaard Arminian for three reasons: 1. His "commitment to universal access to the highest things, over and against belief in double predestination or Christ's limited atonement for the elect." 2. "His commitment to equal responsibility before the highest things, over and against strong versions of sacerdotalism or spiritual collaboration." 3. His "commitment to *human freedom*, freedom of choice, and what might be called 'true' freedom, over and against fatalistic doctrines of irresistible grace or an overly rationalized account of moral and religious commitment."[2]

First, by commitment to universal access what Jackson implies is Kierkegaard holds that a person "can grasp the highest," namely the universal or religion. One can achieve his or her own salvation. In support Jackson quotes a passage from Kierkegaard's Journal. It reads: "I cannot abandon the thought that every man, however simple he is, however much he may suffer, can nevertheless grasp the highest, namely religion."[3] Jackson also refers to *Philosophical Fragments* as evidence of Kierkegaard's Arminianism. He writes: "Johannes Climacus [the pseudonymous author of *Fragments*] asks 'is it not…worthy of the God to make his covenant with men equally difficult for every human being in every time and place…equally difficult but also equally easy, since the God grants the condition?'"[4] He explicates: "But if Kierkegaard pushes his spiritual egalitarianism so far as to deny any personal variability in the task of accepting the covenant that egalitarianism ceases to be credible."[5]

Second, Jackson argues Kierkegaard is committed to the idea of equality of responsibility. By equality of responsibility he means Kierkegaard sees a person's own responsibility, his or her own choice that is, as that which accepts or rejects God's salvation.

> Faith, hope, and love, for Kierkegaard, are akin to passive potentials in finite individuals. They may not be intrinsic to human nature as such, but they are obtainable by human nature aided by grace; and after the Fall they are certainly warped by sin. Yet even as divine flights, they must be accepted and built up; faith, hope, and love cannot be necessitated—not even by God. Humans are to assume that the potential for love of God and neighbor is present in all human beings; 'true greatness is equally accessible to all,' as Johannes de silentio says in Fear and Trembling.[6]

He further notes:

> Moreover, God is owed 'everything' in that God freely offers the prospective lover a necessary condition for healing his now-warped potential and coming into relation with God. The prospective lover/believer has done nothing to merit this salvation—all are equally undeserving before God's redemptive Word—but the individual remains free to accept or reject the divine invitation. One is accountable for saying 'Yes' or 'No' to the grace extended to all. If this is not so, as Jacob Arminius so clearly saw, then God is responsible for evil. For Kierkegaard, then, God's grace is indispensable but not irresistible, a necessary but not a sufficient condition, for human faith, hope, and love.[7]

Third, by human freedom Jackson means that every person is accountable. But, he claims, "Kierkegaard denies the hegemony of reason." Kierkegaard," he says, "radicalizes Augustine's emphasis on inwardness by accenting the epistemic significance of passion and volition, as well as the epistemic impoverishment of reason, in ethical and religious contexts." "Essential truths, Kierkegaard assures us," he says, "must be apprehended via passionate choice, free choice, rather than abstract reflection."[8]

In response to Jackson I will give three respective replies.

First, Jackson's argument for Kierkegaard's commitment to universal access is a misinterpretation of Kierkegaard's position. Kierkegaard's view of freedom, in as much as it is an access to the universal, does not exclude its dialectical relation with the transcendent, which conditions and permits that access.

Second, contrary to Jackson's claim—that Kierkegaard affirms independence of the human will—Kierkegaard holds that the ability to obtain truth is not inherent in us but in God. Jackson assumes Climacus' statement in *Fragments*—that faith is gift—should be understood in the relative sense. He says in spite of the fact that faith is gift Kierkegaard and his pseudonym claim one can freely accept or reject it. According to Jackson, faith does not come by grace in Kierkegaard but is a gift which one can refuse. "The fact that faith is a 'gift of God' does not settle the issue, since one's acceptance of the gift may be harder or easier depending on one's personal history."

In support of that argument he alludes to a rhetorical question in *Fragments* raised by Climacus: "Is it not worthy of the God to make his covenant with men equally difficult for every human being in every time and place… equally difficult but also equally easy, since the God grants the condition?" What Jackson polemically uncovers is the word: condition. He defines it as bearing the meaning of autonomy.

But Jackson's interpretation is misguided. The fact is, when Climacus states God gives the condition, he means one also receives the truth. Let me elaborate.

In *Fragments* Kierkegaard/Climacus writes:

> Now inasmuch as the learner exists [*er til*], he is indeed created, and, accordingly, God must have given him the condition for understanding the truth (for otherwise he previously would have been merely animal, and that teacher who gave him the condition along with the truth would make him a human being for the first time).[9]

His argument is when a person is created he or she is given the truth and the condition to know it. Thus one always has the truth. A person is "not outside the truth" but only polemically against it. Contrary to Jackson and others who assume Kierkegaard's anthropological contention—that one can have the truth if he or she wishes as long as the person ceases to oppose it—Kierkegaard makes an analogical comparison between the biblical truth of God's natural revelation in the world and Socratic recollection. All of his alleged arguments in support of the self/freedom and opposing views against Hegelian universal and others serve to reveal necessary inference to God's absolute existence.[10]

Third, Kierkegaard holds one is in reliance on the creator as the infinite ground of faith without undermining the finite objectivity of his or her existence. There is unique and incomprehensible involvement on the part of the creator in human striving towards faith. He admits grace is above merit and our freedom is always contextualized and subject to God's authority.

The place where we uncover that view is his *For Self-Examination*. There we find Kierkegaard's revealing conclusive statement about grace. He writes: "I am deeply and humbly aware that if I am ever saved I will be saved by grace." Judging from his view of salvation as *sola gratia* and to dismiss all others alluding to Arminian view he bequeaths to the German reformer Martin Luther.

> At that time there appeared a man from God and with faith, Martin Luther; with faith (for truly this required faith) or by faith he established faith in its rights. His life expressed works—let us never forget that—but he said: A person is saved by faith alone.[11]

He then gives a long religious prose in regard to the given doctrine.

> But what happened? There is always a secular mentality that no doubt wants to have the name of being Christian but wants to become Christian as cheaply as possible. This secular mentality became aware of Luther. It listened; for safety's sake it listened once again lest it should have heard wrongly; there-upon it said, 'Excellent! This is something for us. Luther says it depends on faith alone. He himself does not say that his life expresses works, and since he is now dead it is no longer an actuality. So we take his words, his doctrine—and we are free from all works—long live Luther! *Wer nicht liebt Weiber, Wein, Gesang / Er wird ein Narr sein Leben lang* [Who loves not women, wine, and song / He is a fool his whole life long]. This is the meaning of Luther's life, this man of God who, in keeping with the times, reformed Christianity. Even though not everyone took Luther in vain in such a downright secular way—in every human being there is an inclination *either* to want to be meritorious when it comes to works *or*, when faith and grace are to be emphasized, also to want to be free from works as far as possible. Indeed, 'man,' this rational creation of God, certainly does not let himself be fooled; he is not a peasant coming to market, he has his eyes open. 'No, it's one or the other,' says man. 'If it is to be *works*—fine, but then I must also ask for the legitimate yield I have coming from my works, so that they are meritorious. If it is to be *grace*—fine, but then I must also ask to be free from works—otherwise it surely is not grace. If it is to be works and nevertheless grace, that is indeed foolishness.' Yes, that is indeed foolishness; that would also be true Lutheranism; that would

indeed be Christianity. Christianity's requirement is this: your life should express works as strenuously as possible; then one thing more is required—that you humble yourself and confess. But my being saved is nevertheless grace."[12]

The Lutheran doctrine of salvation contains two elements: grace and merit. But merit has a different meaning than how it was commonly understood in the Middle Ages in Luther. According to Kierkegaard:

> The error of Middle Ages, meritoriousness, was abhorred. But when one scrutinizes the matter more deeply, it is easy to see that people had perhaps an even greater notion that works are meritorious than did the Middle Ages, but they applied *grace* in such a way that they freed themselves from works. Having abolished works, they could not very well be tempted to regard as something meritorious the works they did not do. Luther wished to take 'meritoriousness' away from works and apply them somewhat differently—namely, in the direction of witnessing for the truth; the secular mentality, which understood Luther perfectly took meritoriousness away altogether— including the works.[13]

What Kierkegaard is suggesting here is, even though faith (grace) is gift it has to be received. By doing that he is not revealing an Arminian view. He simply and correctly points to faith's dual conditions of given-ness and reception wherein he equally speaks of the absolutely necessary being of faith as God's gift to humanity. Hence he views faith within the broader truth of God's absoluteness over and against human freedom and merit.

Incidentally one could perceive Kierkegaard as an Arminian if he or she sees his abhorred emphasis on human freedom and individuality. After all, the main intention behind his works is to convey the objectivity of human life against the lifeless concept of humanity. But he is an adamant Lutheran when it comes to the grace-freedom relation. For him the relation is collaboration between God and the self wherein the absolute distinction is kept. God is infinite and humans are finite. Grace imposes on freedom. Yet, it does not tear asunder God's primacy.

There are two important points to make about Kierkegaard's concept of freedom. First, freedom has two dimensions: historical (freedom) and eternal (necessity). He calls the historical an occasion of finite category. The historical implies limitations. It points to the ambiguity of human life. The most elaborate thinking or observation does not attain its full meaning. Freedom conditions existence but not its essence (contra Heidegger, Sartre and so on). It is an aspect of life. Although we are free, our freedom is in service to God. It is the condition of worship. Freedom is anchored in one's religious obligation of obedience and love. Hence he exhorts in his *Works of Love*:

> There is only one whom a person can with the truth of eternity love more than himself [as a free being]—that is God. Therefore it does not say, 'You shall love God as yourself' but says, 'You shall love the Lord your God with all your heart and all your soul and all your mind.' A person should love God unconditionally in obedience and love him in adoration. You shall love God in unconditional obedience."[14]

According to Kierkegaard, Christianity assumes one understands the purpose of life as an obligation of loving God. Christian faith points to self-denial and suffering.

Second, freedom points to others. A Christian life stands in relation to others in self-denial and sacrifice. Hence, the meaning of human life conveys a different meaning from the one which is commonly thought, namely it is independent from God and others thus free from loving and caring. Kierkegaard stresses a life of freedom entails love of suffering. It points to loving God and caring for other. Life and caring/love are inevitably connected. He writes:

> One who truly loves does not seek his own. With regard to his 'own,' he knows nothing about the claims of strict law or of justice, not even the claims of equity; neither does he know anything about an exchange that erotic love makes, which also knows how to watch out lest it be tricked. No, the one who truly loves knows how to do only one thing: how to be tricked, to be deceived, to give everything away without getting the least in return.[15]

He further states:

> Free heart is required for love or giving oneself in love, this heart must not belong to anyone else or to anything else; yes, even the hand that gives it away must be free. This heart, free as it is, will then find total freedom in giving itself away. Nothing—the bird you release from your hand, the arrow from the slackened bow string, the bent branch that snaps back—nothing is as free as the free heart when it freely gives itself away.[16]

Against philosophical notions of freedom as independence and autonomy Kierkegaard lays its peculiar understanding as death to self. The idea is best reflected in the words of a German pastor and theologian Dietrich Bonhoeffer writes:

There is a reversal of all human existence, in the very fact that Jesus only 'is there for others.' Jesus' 'being for others' is the experience of transcendence! Only through this liberation from self, through this 'being-for-others' unto death, do omnipotence, omniscience, and omnipresence come into being. Faith is participating in this being of Jesus. Our relationship to God is a new life in 'being there for others,' through participation in the being of Jesus.[17]

Second, there also is a cognitive affirmation of one's relation to the transcendent. For Kierkegaard the essence of being is *being-in-relation* to the absolute other—God. Existence pre-attests to God's being.[18] Human life existentially affirms the transcendent and validates God's affinity with the world. It affirms the dichotomy between God and the human in which the transcendent subject takes the upper hand over and against the objectivity of human existence. Kierkegaard affirms a life's subjection to God's preponderance. Freedom is refuted in every occasion by God's initiative.

That does not mean he refutes a human life altogether. In fact, he strongly advocates human individuality. His uncompromising emphasis on the significance of human life or existence is shown in his strong opposition to all forms of objective thinking about truth—Hegel's philosophy being the main one. He sees Hegel or Hegelian philosophy as having "sought to relate all things through the intellect, to overcome all antitheses through pure thought." Kierkegaard's problem with the German philosopher, as we saw, is he "relates to everything in general and nothing in particular."[19]

Even though Kierkegaard stresses dialectic, his method is one of distinction or differentiation. While he acknowledges the absoluteness of transcendence he does not depreciate humanity. While he appreciates the infinite as that which stands beyond human reach, he does not refute the significance of the historical. As Daniel Price promptly notes:

Kierkegaard sought to appreciate the significance of divine revelation by pointing out the naturally occurring distance between God and humanity. Unlike Hegel's dialectic, Kierkegaard's was a dialectic of intellectual humility. It was humble because it was suspicious of any wholly consistent system of thought. It was humble because any possible synthesis between God and humanity, between time and eternity, came from divine initiative and not from human thought.[20]

In modernity freedom succeeded in disavowing the transcendent. For example, in naturalism freedom repudiates the transcendent in forms of expansive pantheism and dualism. Here, we may once more refer to Kant as an example.

Kant's natural philosophy greatly influenced the ways in which human beings would view the transcendent and its relation to the world. Kant's dualism, for example, separates God and the world and bids us to turn toward the self. Consequently, ever since the coming of Kant's philosophy the social order has been subject to the dominance of humanity with zero tolerance of the transcendent. According to Kant, the world is a permanent service to humanity and constantly subjects to its dominance.

But according to Kierkegaard the Kantian concept of humanity fails to give a sufficient account of the transcendent as an object. God for Kant is an "object of presentation" as opposed to being a reality. According to Kant, a presentation is not an object. Instead it is an idea, an idea of a necessary being.[21]

> And here we need to clarify what we mean by the expression *an object of presentations*. Appearances themselves are nothing but sensible presentations. But presentations in themselves must not in the same way be regarded as objects (outside our power of presentation). What, then, do we mean when we talk about an object corresponding to, and hence also distinct from, cognition? We can easily see that this object must be thought only as something as such $=x$. [22]

In contrast to Kant's view, Kierkegaard holds the transcendent is not an abstract idea but an actuality. The ideal of the transcendent is thought by virtue of there being correlation between God and human beings. Religious consciousness of the divine and our constant colliding with that truth, as shown in *Fragments* for instance, imply God is an object. God is the ultimate reference point of human consciousness, but our religious consciousness is mediated through freedom. Our religious consciousness then is symbolic of our historical participation in the transcendent. For Kierkegaard, our relation to the divine is "the central relation." And that relation surpasses historical and cultural moments as the absolute reference point. In the words of a Dutch philosopher, Herman Dooyeweerd, the transcendent and the distinction between divine universality (transcendent) and human consciousness lies between those two dialectical moments of experience in an undivided unity between God and the self.[23]

According to Dooyeweerd, the certainty of that moment normally derives in three ways: faith, feeling, and representation or thought. First, regarding faith it is a reaction to that which imposes on humanity, namely the transcendent. Second, with respect to feeling there is an object or external cause. Third, with respect to representation it is a consciousness of something objective.

Philosophy, says Dooyeweerd, transforms these representations into what are called concepts. But the content of their truth remains unchanged. Representations contain sensible forms and configurations, what we call images. Those images directly relate to our senses.

There are two stages to sense of feeling: immediate and mediate. The former is the external and the latter is the internal. And what we normally refer to as religious representations are metaphors containing those two elements. For example, the concept of the Trinity—God the Father, God the Son, God the Holy Spirit—is a metaphorical concept. It is metaphorical in that we do not have its true conceptual understanding. We can only give symbolic interpretation because it has a non-literal meaning.

The Trinity, though a reality, is understood at the sacrifice of our finite rationality. The same notion applies to other biblical records such as: creation, Incarnation and the resurrection of Jesus. One can only understand those concepts in forms of representation or images which convert to concepts which are rationally recognizable simply because they are objects.

Returning to the question of God-freedom relation, then, Kierkegaard believes the categorical experience of the unity of God and humanity occurs as a result of God's revelation. Freedom is grounded in one's historical relation with the transcendent. What that relation implies is our genetic or natural knowledge of the divine.

Here, I find Paul Tillich to be helpful. According to Tillich:

> Reason is the precondition of faith; faith is the act in which reason reaches ecstatically beyond itself. This is the opposite side of their being within each other. Man's reason is finite; it moves within finite relations when dealing with the universe and with man himself. All cultural activities in which man perceives his world and those in which he shapes his world have this character of finitude. Therefore, they are not matters of infinite concern. But reason is not bound to its own finitude. It is aware of it and, in so doing, rises above it. Man experiences a belonging to the infinite which, however, is neither a part of himself nor something in his power. It must grasp him, and if it does, it is a matter of infinite concern.

He further states:

> Man is finite, man's reason lives in preliminary concerns; but man is also aware of his potential infinity, and this awareness appears as his ultimate concern, as faith. If reason is grasped by an ultimate concern, it is driven beyond itself; but it does not cease to be reason, finite reason. The ecstatic experience of an ultimate concern does not destroy the structure of reason. Ecstasy is fulfilled, not denied, rationality. Reason can be fulfilled only if it is driven beyond the limits of its finitude, and experiences

the presence of the ultimate, the holy. *Reason is the presupposition of faith, and faith is the fulfillment of reason.* Faith as the state of ultimate concern is reason in ecstasy. There is no conflict between the nature of faith and the nature of reason; they are within each other.[24]

According to Tillich, God's revelation has a motive. It reveals the unity of the self and the divine which is not arbitrary but "metaphysically ultimate": it motivates a person towards faith.

As we saw, Kierkegaard too acknowledges human beings' natural knowledge of God. In *Fragments*—the work which elicits and strengthens apologetics—the pseudonym Johannes Climacus attempts to vindicate the truth by exploring the basic ideas of Christian theism. He expresses the primary notion to be the religious knowledge of the transcendent.

It is true that the evidence of Christianity, such as the Incarnation, resurrection and so on cannot be valid outside faith since reason (evidence) and faith collide. But he argues the vindication and acceptance of biblical events of the past are two different things. The vindication of those events, he says, is historically achievable even though that does not necessarily lead to faith. Those claims, he exhorts, are justifiable in concordance with our given knowledge/rational-experience of the divine.

That discovery in *Fragments* and his other works displays a new revelation concerning freedom. It plumbs Kierkegaard is not a subjectivist who rejects concordance between God and humanity, as some have thought. For example the philosopher Emmanuel Levinas argues Kierkegaard deprives objectivity, which otherwise connects the self to the transcendent.

> Kierkegaard rehabilitated subjectivity—the unique, the singular—with incomparable strength. But in protesting against the absorption of subjectivity by Hegel's universality, he bequeathed to the history of philosophy and exhibitionistic, immodest subjectivity that completely naked subjectivity that, in its desire to avoid losing itself in the universal, rejects all form.[25]

But a thorough study of Kierkegaard's subjectivity reveals otherwise. Contrary to Levinas' view, Kierkegaard's main concern is not with Hegel's universalizing philosophy. Instead, it is with the distortion of the truth by the church in his time.[26]

Indeed one must admit of Kierkegaard's criticism of Hegel's universalizing philosophy. He declares Hegel's system threatens freedom and existence with becoming completely imbibed into objective universality. But, despite his concern—which hazardously impinges on the problem of individuality—his greater concern is with the problem of recalcitrant and rebellious Christendom in his time (in Denmark).

Second, with respect to Levinas' claim—that there is no objectivity in Kierkegaard—nothing can be further from the truth. As we have noted, historical objectivity (i.e., freedom, being, faith and so on) is not at all neglected in subjectivity. On the contrary, he concurs human beings are naturally impregnated with the knowledge of the transcendent. He declares in *Fragments*: "faith and the historical fact are entirely commensurate" and that "the absolute fact is also historical [fact, truth]." How the two intersect is not discussed in detail. But nonetheless he promotes complete interplay between the subjective (self) and the objective (transcendent).[27]

Human reason or will does not wield faith. Faith has the primacy over reason. That does not mean reason should be abandoned. Faith does not deprive subjectivity in its bare nakedness in Kierkegaard as Levinas and others contort. Unfortunately, what they overlook is his way of limiting reason to a supporting role by safeguarding the unconditionality of the transcendent from historical contingencies.[28]

Freedom and Necessity

Here, we turn to the question concerning the relation between freedom and necessity, otherwise known as subjective and objective. The core of the problem is its dual nature. Thus, our attempt is to mark the point of intersection and divergence between the two in relation to our overall discussion of God-freedom relation.

We will begin by saying the self in Kierkegaard is a being. That being is free. The self is free by virtue of being conscious of its reality. In other words, being is constituted by its cognitive awareness.

According to Kierkegaard, there is a religious dimension to our existence. The proof is our choices are never un-constrained choices. They are not independent decisions. Human choices are free but necessitated decisions. The singularity of human freedom never possesses the legitimate property of universality apart from its dependence on divine exteriority. But because there also is a formal relation between God and the self, that relation is one of polarization and unity. Our voluntary choice is always embodied with the involuntary determination. Here I find a philosopher Paul Ricoeur to be helpful.

According to Ricoeur, the cultural elements which influence choice, such as motivations and historical conditions, are not only that by which one is actual but also bear limitations that constrain choices. While choices are actual and voluntary, they do not fail to reflect toward their relation to the transcendent doxologically. Our moments of choice are tied to God's higher determination. Therefore the voluntary and the involuntary between God and the self is the "organ of one's action" and also "the condition of a person's being."[29] The voluntary (relative) and the involuntary (absolute) unite the action of the subject.

Kierkegaard, like Heidegger, Sartre and others, sees freedom as the core of our existence. He also shares their perception that freedom has roots in temporality. Thus it has origin in non-being. That means we are not necessary beings because what has come into being is temporal. Therefore, the unity of necessity and freedom is a relation of temporality in the sense it belongs to the world of time and ideal.[30]

> Changes are possible only in time. Therefore time is something actual. Time is indeed something actual, viz., the actual form of inner intuition. It therefore has subjective reality in regard to inner experience; i.e., I actually have the presentation of time and of my determinations in time.[31]

But necessity is something different. It is not change. Its meaning contradicts temporality. Whereas time or freedom is an empirical reality, necessity is beyond the empirical. To borrow Kant's words:

> Time retains its empirical reality as condition of all our experiences. Only absolute reality must be denied of time. Time is nothing but the form of our inner intuition. If we take away from time [the qualification that it is] the special condition of our sensibility, then the concept of time vanishes as well; time attaches not to objects themselves, but merely to the subject intuiting them. But what causes this objection to be raised so unanimously, and raised, moreover, by those who nonetheless cannot think of any plausible objection against the doctrine that space is ideal, is the following. They had no hope of establishing apodeictically that space is real absolutely; for they are confronted by idealism, according to which the actuality of external objects is incapable of strict proof. By contrast, the actuality of the object of our inner sense (the actuality of myself and of my state) is directly evident through consciousness. External objects might be a mere illusion; but the object of inner sense is, in their opinion, undeniably something actual.[32]

According to Kierkegaard, necessity is an ideal (eternal). In his words: "necessity is." It is not bound to the historical, although one may still conceive it as change by virtue of its own final predication, namely by its non-objectivity.[33]

Hence freedom is an imperfection. According to Kierkegaard human nature's imperfection is: it has history or past. In other words, freedom came into being. The way it is expressed is: "The coming into existence [being, freedom] is possibility, a possibility that for nature [or freedom] is its whole actuality."[34]

But one may rightly ask: is not the past something necessary since it cannot change? His answer is: the unchanging character of the past is not the same quality of necessity. The actual "thus and so" of the past cannot become different. Any and every past occurrence took place as a result of coming into existence. Hence they cannot be necessity. Being is time bound. It is temporality. Being is by virtue of non-necessity.

The word necessity however denotes the eternal. He writes: "It is the perfection of the eternal to have no history, and of all that is, only the eternal has absolutely no history." Being's origin is in temporality. History then is temporal since it is a being.[35] It is also is the case with respect to future occurrences. The future, he says, "has not yet occurred."

> But it is not, because of that, less necessary than the past, in as much as the past did not become necessary by having occurred, but, on the contrary, by *having occurred, it demonstrated that it was not necessary* [for that which exists in necessity is eternal in nature]. If the past had become necessary, the opposite conclusion could not be drawn with respect to the future [for in such case, the future must already be in existence if they existed in necessity], but on the contrary it would follow that the future could also be necessary. To want to predict the future (prophecy) and to want to understand the necessity of the past are altogether identical, and only the prevailing fashion makes one seem more plausible than the other to a particular generation. The past has indeed come into existence, coming into existence is the change, in freedom, in becoming actuality.[36]

Suffice it to say, temporality has an important meaning in Kierkegaard, in relation to the past in particular and to the world in general. It points to their freedom. He sees God as the only necessary being outside the world which cannot come into existence. God, he says, is the only necessary being. Arguing in the same traditions of Anselm, Descartes, Kant and others who have formulated ontological arguments of the transcendent/necessity/necessary being, Kierkegaard shows no pretense in metaphysically conveying the same notion.

> If the past had become necessary, then it would not belong to freedom anymore—that is, belong to that which came into existence. Freedom would then be in dire

straits, something to laugh about and to weep over, since it would bear responsibility for what did not belong to it, would bring forth what necessity would devour, and freedom itself would be an illusion and coming into existence no less an illusion; freedom would become witchcraft and coming into existence a false alarm.[37]

He further relates:

Coming into existence is a change, but since the necessary is always related to itself in the same way, it cannot be changed at all. All coming into existence is a *suffering* (*Liden*), and the necessary cannot suffer, cannot suffer the suffering of actuality—namely, that the possible (not merely the possible that is excluded but even the possibility that is accepted) turns out to be nothing the moment it become actual, for possibility is annihilated by actuality. Precisely, by coming into existence, everything that comes into existence demonstrates that it is not necessary, for the only thing that cannot come into existence is the necessary, because the necessary *is*.[38]

Human consciousness, he argues, always precedes the transcendent leap in seeing that underlying distinction between human freedom and divine necessity.[39]

Nonetheless, he emphasizes that leap is the will's act of choosing and that one must not have a false notion that it is thought's logically determined necessity as, for instance, is the case in Hegelian philosophy. In Hegel or Hegelian philosophy the eternal (Absolute Spirit) is an immanent object which is not the final destiny in and of world history as expressed in Christianity. Hegelian logic opposes Kierekgaardian a priori religious principles or concepts by which our rationality functions. Kierkegaard contends human thought can only describe things as they are in their pre-empted meanings which are constituted within thought's logical framework.

In similar manner, reason correctly identifies the categories of the eternal and temporal as conforming to their original categories. For example, one does not define an eternal object as a temporal object or vice versa. In spite of claiming the retrieval of the eternal spirit in temporality (history), Hegel, says Kierkegaard, must be aware that the world has an external tie to the world outside history. The fact that the world has an external tie, he says, is what ensures human freedom. That external relation secures uncertain matters, such as human finitude and social chaos. Thus in response to Hegel's crippling logic, which historically constitutes the eternal (necessity) and deprives all possible solutions to human predicaments, Kierkegaard writes:

What would this mean? (In such case) *Possibility and actuality are not different in essence but in being.* How could there be formed from this heterogeneity a unity that would be necessity, which is not a qualification of being but of essence, since the essence of the necessary is to be. In such a case, possibility and actuality, in becoming necessity, would become an absolutely different essence, which is no change, and, becoming necessity or the necessary, would become the one and only that precludes coming into existence, which is just as impossible as it is self-contradictory…Necessity stands all by itself. Nothing whatever comes into existence by way of necessity, no more than necessity comes into existence or anything incoming into existence becomes the necessary. Nothing whatever exists (*er til*) because it is necessary, but the necessary exists because it is necessary or because the necessary is. The actual is no more necessary than the possible, for the necessary is absolutely different from both.[40]

Contrary to the Hegelian concept of being/freedom—which introduces false definition of the eternal, something transformed into an onto-logic that abstractly unites the God with humanity—Kierkegaard asserts their absolute distinction. Contrary to Hegelian logic, which conveys ambivalence in human freedom, Kierkegaard expresses its reality. Whereas in Hegel the subject performs the double role of freedom and necessary—hence obscuring the transcendent—Kierkegaard affirms God's higher vantage point.

In a journal he wrote, Kierkegaard shows his distaste for abstraction of freedom and expresses his heightened sense of the historical. He does it by virtue of seeing human consciousness as real experience of the transcendent. He identifies the eternal in distinction to the world. In the next entry, he goes as far as stating that the next proceeding task of consciousness is to focus on existence which directs all thinking to "genuine anthropological contemplation" of the absolute being.[41]

What serve as pointers of God's being in him are certain existential experience. One of those is "despair." But, unlike Hegel and others, he applies it to actual human life. He says despair is what is experienced in losing the first state of innocence and under sin doubts whether he or she can return to the first state of unity with God. Contrary to Hegel and Hegelian philosophy which fails to account for human emotions objectively, Kierkegaard claims it is the most concretely experienced elements in one's life along with anxiety and guilt.

For that reason, Kierkegaard, for example, would oppose the radical ontology of human death as the end of being advocated by Heidegger and Heideggerians. According to Heidegger, the cause of human anxiety is the fear of death. But according to Kierkegaard, anxiety is caused, not so much by one's fear of dying, but instead by the uncertainty beyond death. Kierkegaard's concept of anxiety goes beyond Heideggerian ontology and imposes meta-physical consideration: it leads to soul-searching and preparation for eternity. Unlike Heidegger and others, Kierkegaard's ethical consideration of human anxiety points to the fact that human emotions such as anxiety and others manifest our inadequate state of "religious" condition.

Philosophers such as Heidegger and others define those emotions as formal existential qualities, the underlying structure of what it means to be human. For example, Heidegger contends human emotions reveal our present state or condition as "fleeing" from best insight or knowledge as to what we are to do about facing death without the need of ethical considerations, such as the one Kierkegaard imposes: life after death.

Heidegger declares one should not flee from anxiety. Instead of running away from fear of death, one should always choose a project in view of that final destiny. One should not sweat the small stuff, he declares. Instead, the awareness of death should free a person from constraints of life. To live that life of authenticity is to shape one's life despite problems and limitations. One should shape life so that it becomes something worth talking about in the future. Anxiety is a way of escaping from the awareness of what one sees or knows as the imposing knowledge (death).[42]

In our next and final discussion, we will discuss the problem of absolute distinction and historical unity as the criterion of upholding the God-freedom relation. We will argue that criterion is exhibited in the absolute paradox of God's Incarnation in Jesus Christ. We will argue that the absolute paradox of the God-man is the paradigm of understanding the relation as one of essential distinction and historical connection.

The Incarnation and the God-Freedom Relation

In this section we explore the meaning of God's Incarnation as absolute paradox. The intent is to demonstrate that God's Incarnation must be seen as the basis of the God-freedom irony.

As we mentioned, Kierkegaard protests Hegelian or any other abstraction of thought that attempts to reconcile the God-world relation as a single unity without distinction. One reason is it obscures the transcendent identity of God and humanity's historical place in the world.

For Kierkegaard the Incarnation is an impenetrable fact. It stands at the "un-crossable" border which the "thought itself cannot think."[43] It borders between the eternal and the human, a place which philosophers have called "horizon." Its meaning depicts mystery, a point at which heaven and earth perhaps meet without subjecting to our rational comprehension.

> The human spirit is struck by the inexplicable fact of God's revelation; it encounters this fact, this phenomenon. It simply misunderstands it when it tries to approach this phenomenon of God's revelation and make it comprehensible in terms of historical science. God's revelation in Christ is an un-crossable boundary of our spirit, our reason; our science, our thought, but it is a boundary for us because it is absurd to our thought. That means it is something that can be proven impossible and thus certainly one-existent.[44]

If one is to call the world (historical) a necessity and abstractly unite it with the eternal, as in the case of Hegel for instance, then one encounters a problem: the identity and the redemptive work of the God-man is neutralized.

For Kierkegaard, the Incarnation represents the ultimate paradox of the absolute distinction and historical unity between God and the world. Unlike Hegel—who emphasizes the singular unity of God and the world— Kierkegaard demonstrates the objectivity of God's being and humanity. He does it to show the event reveals God's love towards people.

> The history of Christ's sufferings belongs to the history of the sufferings of mankind, by virtue of the passionate love which Christ manifests and reveals. The interpretation of Christ's death on the cross as an atoning event in the framework of the question of human guilt is the central part of this universal significance.[45]

Unlike Hegel and others, Kierkegaard believes God's Incarnation in Jesus Christ is a true event not conducive to logic. Logic cannot grasp it. Reason does not apprehend it. It is an "offense" to human understanding in laying bare our rational capacity.

Incidentally, for Kierkegaard the God-freedom relation demands the same principle as that of human perception: "an objective necessity of the determination" of their identity in the subjective. It commands us to step beyond the event, as it were, to see outside its ironic form at the new realm which sees no demarcation. It demands our leap beyond the empirical and that we be carried into the world of the transcendent. What our discussion here really establishes is his view that there is religious interpersonal relation at play between God and humanity and it is only by transcendent belief that one negates the absurdity of the synthesis and brings the dialectic into appropriation.

How he validates that point is found in *Fragments*. There, he argues one could not know an object without the object being conditioned by its a priori concept. For example, one does not know an object is stone without ideally assuming it as such. The argument goes like this: "I never reason in conclusion to existence, but I reason in conclusion from existence. For example I do not demonstrate that a stone exists but that something which exists is a stone."[46]

What he is arguing here is for the unavoidable correlation between the object and our understanding. For Kierkegaard the case concerning the Incarnation and the God-freedom relation is perceived in no different manner than through our a priori concepts of those matters. His view is that even at the rational level we are capable of appropriating the transcendent. As he declares, we are never outside the truth (God's being).

In supporting his position, Kierkegaard makes an analogical assertion. He argues there is correlation between Christianity and the Greek concept of recollection. He claims both views claim our natural knowledge of the truth. The difference is: "The Socratic principle emphasizes the idea of immortality of the [human] soul whereas Christianity stresses creation."[47] He claims although their arguments differ in presupposition, they are common in seeing the relation of historical unity between them.

What that entails is of God's immanence in the world. That precise relation is ultimately reflected in Jesus Christ, the absolute paradox. As the Incarnation of God in Jesus depicts the absoluteness and historical relation of the transcendent to humanity, so does the relation between God and humanity (freedom). The person of Jesus Christ, the absolute paradox of the God-man, is the archetypical form of which the relation between God's absoluteness and our freedom bears its prototype. All of the experienced ironies in life within the finitude-infinitude relation are express images of the Incarnation, which is the unity of God and human in a single person without disparaging their identities. The Incarnation is the ultimate form of the welded relation between God and history most intimately and profoundly expressed. Therefore, it is the basis of all of the paradoxes in life.

The Incarnation demonstrates itself at two levels: historical and absolute. At the historical level, the Incarnation is subject to logic. But, logic's limit is shown at the dividing line between rationality and faith. At the absolute level, the Incarnation is no longer a paradox since here logic is no longer the standard but must surrender to the eternal.

Is God Free? Barth and Moltmann on Divine Freedom

In Kierkegaard's view, freedom as both independence and being bound reflects the nature of God's own being. For example, he sees God's freedom as that which forms the qualified unity of various aspects of his eternal character together with other aspects (i.e., love and justice). Those aspects are revealed by different actions God takes. In order to explore this problem—for the purpose of further clarifying the meaning of freedom and its relation to the transcendent—we will present two representative thinkers whose views directly oppose one another. They are Karl Barth and Jürgen Moltmann. We will show their reasoning and offer a Kierkegaardian corrective. We will contend the voluntary and involuntary aspects of freedom in Kierkegaard and that those aspects also reflect the nature of God's own freedom.

First, we will discuss Moltmann's nominalist position against the backdrop of Barth's less nominalist view. Moltmann argues even though Barth tries to escape what he calls "the nominalist doctrine of *potential absoluta*," he still shows a "nominalist fringe."[48] I will examine their arguments and give an account of what I believe is Kierkegaard's own take on the problem.

In *The Trinity and the Kingdom* Moltmann states:

The question which we have to discuss in considering the theology of the divine passion (Christ's suffering) is the question of God's freedom. Is the suffering God free or is he a prisoner of his own history? What is the reason behind the passion of God that makes him suffer with his creation and his people? What freedom can be called divine freedom?[49]

He goes on to say:

The initial answer is to be found in the nominalist doctrine of decree: God is free. He is compelled to nothing. He can do and leave undone whatever he likes. His creative and suffering love is founded on his groundless decision.[50]

Referring to Karl Barth, he states:

Karl Barth tried to get over the nominalist doctrine of *potential absoluta*, especially in his criticism of Luther. None the less, in his doctrine of God's primordial decision a nominalist fringe still remains.[51]

In order to prove his claim, Moltmann cites a passage from Barth's *Christian Dogmatics*. There Barth contends:

> He (God) could have remained satisfied with Himself and with the impassible glory and blessedness of His own inner life. But he did not do so. He elected man as a covenant–partner. This God has no need of us. This God is self-sufficient. This God knows perfect beatitude in Himself. He is not under any need of constraint. It takes place in an inconceivably free over-flowing of His goodness if he determines to co-exist with a reality distinct from Himself, with the world of creatures, ourselves. God in His love elects another to fellowship with Himself. First and foremost this means that God makes a self-election in favour of this other. He ordains that He should not be entirely self-sufficient as He might be.[52]

In response to Barth's claim, Moltmann asks:

> What concept of liberty is Barth applying to God here? Is this concept of absolute freedom of choice not a threat to God's truth and goodness? Could God really be content with his 'impassible glory? Does God really not need those whom in the suffering of his love he loves unendingly?[53]

Here, the argument which Moltmann gives in response to Barth is for the singularity of God's divine essence. He points out there can be no contradiction between being and action in him. If God is one, he states, that is if his being is a unity, then his revelation must comply with his nature.

According to Moltmann:

> If God is the truth in that he corresponds entirely to himself, then this revelation can only be true if he entirely corresponds to himself in that revelation. That is to say, not to reveal himself and to be contented with his untouched glory would be a contradiction of himself. And if he himself determines not to be sufficient for himself (although he could be so), then there is after all a contradiction between his nature before and after this decision; and this would mean a contradiction between his nature and his revelation. The reasoning 'God could' or 'God could have' is inappropriate. It does not lead to an understanding of God's freedom. God's freedom can never contradict the truth which he himself is.[54]

His biblical argument is from 2 Timothy 2:13: "He remains faithful for he cannot deny himself." He also suggests 1 John 1:15: "God is light and in him is no darkness."

Moltmann's concept of the unity of God's being might sound convincing. After all, how could one imagine a God whose nature is inconsistent? No one would disparage God as a being of unity. God's actions not only derive from but equally correspond to his will. However, his interpretation of Barth's claim—that God could have remained sufficient but elected the other reality to co-exist as contradictory—is misguided.

Barth's assertion, that God could have alone existed without creating or electing the other, but in his love determined to co-exist with the world, does not mitigate or blacken God's self-sufficiency. Instead, it demonstrates God's dynamic freedom, which either could or could not choose to co-exist with the world. In other words, he is showing God's creative nature, not depicting contradiction.

Barth believes in God's self-sufficient nature. He also sees certain aspects (i.e., desire, wish, love and so on) as a factor which contributes to his actions. To illustrate: the question of whether one should have or not have a child is a choice as opposed to being a necessity. In the same manner, God's revelation is a choice, says Barth, to relate to the other and not a way of fulfilling a need. Therefore, it does not demonstrate contradiction in his being.

Therefore, Moltmann's claim against Barth: "If God is the truth in that he corresponds entirely to himself, not to reveal himself and be contended with his untouched glory would be a contradiction of himself" is irrelevant. His argument has a false beginning in that it links God's revelation with the notion that he could be compelled in Barth. Barth makes no such claim.

Contrary to Moltmann's view, Barth sees God's being as having no need of constraint. Revelation for him is God's free act, a "groundless decision." "God is not compelled to nothing." He has no need to love (the other). His creation and love for humanity is not out of need or some inadequacy in his being, but simply out of his eternal desire and freedom.

For Barth God's freedom does not separate itself from the unity. God's unity or his unified essence is at the core of Barth's theology. Contrary to Moltmann and others who equate God's freedom with his need, Barth defines divine freedom as liberty of making a choice. Incorrectly, Moltmann sees that as a nominalist fringe in Barth.

What Moltmann mistakenly overlooks is Barth's attempt to reconcile what Moltmann sees as a nominalist fringe with respect to God's eternal freedom. Barth never denies the unity of God's being. He sees no contradiction in God's being and action, as Moltmann and others claim. Contrary to Moltmann's view, Barth does not denote constraint on God's part with respect to his revelation. What he reveals is God's absolute freedom which transcends human thinking. Moltmann depicts it as a constraint in Barth's theology.

From Moltmann's standpoint, God's revelation may imply constraint. For instance, God's love for the world—in which God delivered Christ into suffering—may seem to denote constraint on God's part for the reason that it is the cause of deliverance of his Son into suffering and death. But Barth gives a different view. Revelation is that which God could or needs not to have to achieve.

For Barth, God's revelation is a constraint-free act which derives from his love. It can also be called God's desire (Augustine). To call God's love—demonstrated in the suffering of his Son—anything other than love or desire is to limit his absolute essence. Barth sees God's being or unity as structured so as to hold different privileges which otherwise might be seen as nominalist fringes and contradictions.

As both Moltmann and Barth contend for the unity of God's divine essence, it is Barth who successfully escapes immanentizing God by casting a romantist view (Moltmann). A close look at Barth's concept will tell his concept of unity of freedom and love is much more nuanced than that of Moltmann and others.

However, one must be reminded that Barth opposes both rationalistic and romantic ways of understanding the relation between love and freedom. His method is distinctly dialectical. His dialectic opposes humanistic attempts in theology, which attempts to give a logical solution to the problem of God's being. He exclusively sets the relation between freedom and love around his religious or theological concept of the Incarnation.

As Price correctly points out:

> In place of a theology based on immanence Barth chose a theology of 'encounter.' In the place of intellectual systems, Barth chose to focus on particular existence and actions. Both rationalistic and romantic systems fell under the sweeping 'No' of Barth's dialectical theology. The resounding 'No' of the *Epistles to the Romans* is Kierkegaardian to the extent that it denies the human possibility of knowing God apart from the Incarnation.[55]

Price is right in saying that Barth's understanding of the paradox of the God-man is taken from his study of Kierkegaard. For that reason, Barth, just as did Kierkegaard, guarded against natural theology. He was being suspicious of any "intellectual apprehension of God apart from incarnation and revelation."[56]

According to Price:

> Kierkegaard was fond of stating: 'truth is subjectivity.' The most important kind of truth, according to Kierkegaard, can be attained only through taking a count of the

person as an existing subject [in relation to the transcendent]. No one is able to think universal thoughts apart from their prior individual existence.[57]

Here, Price sees subjectivity as depicting different notions about the self and its relation to the transcendent. To be in relation with God is to be aware of it inwardly in the abyss of inner world, apart from objective understanding.

> 'Truth is subjectivity' therefore expresses a supreme skepticism toward philosophical systems, especially those which tend to blur the separation between subject and object, between thinking and being. For Kierkegaard, 'The systematic Idea is the identity of subject and object, the unity of thought and being. Existence, on the other hand, is their separation.'[58]

Price further writes:

> Barth does not deny that philosophical systems are capable of some degree of understanding about God; he does deny, however, that systems are compatible with the Christian means of knowing God. Philosophical systems may have some application to the God-relationship within the self; but this has little to do with Christianity, argues Kierkegaard. In Christianity, the God-relation is always 'something outside the individual, the individual does not find edification by finding the God-relationship within himself, but relates himself to something outside himself to find edification.[59]

Returning to the problem of freedom, then, Barth's creative view of love and freedom as unity in God is discovered in creation-redemption dialectic. First, below is his own thesis on the topic:

> Creation and redemption are inseparably conjoined in the one work of grace. If creation comes first, it is no more a prelude than redemption an afterthought, for it is itself the actualization of God's grace. Creation is the outer and redemption the inner side of the one free and loving decision and action of God.[60]

As we mentioned in an earlier discussion, for Barth love and freedom, and other divine elements for that matter, are unified aspects in God's single essence. Therefore, no one quality of God can be sacrificed by or oppose other qualities.

Still, there are limitations to Barth's analysis. Even though he is Kierkegaardian when it comes to viewing God-freedom relation as one of an absolute distinction, he fails to point out the single importance of Kierkegaardian subjectivity as the solution to appropriating the supposed freedom-love dichotomy in God.

As we have explored, subjectivity in Kierkegaard means an inward or personal appropriation. That means for him every paradoxical concept, including the Incarnation, finds solution in inner appropriation. Hence, the Incarnation as God's love and justice does not reveal contradiction in his being but unity of God's goodness towards humanity.

For Kierkegaard, unity of love and justice is most apparent in God's Incarnation. In a journal entry, Kierkegaard writes: "At every moment Christ is God just as much as he is man."[61] His view of man as a unity as opposed to a duality affects his view of God as a being with all of his multi-attributes forming that relation.[62] Without rejecting the objectivity of the Incarnation, Kierkegaard emphasizes one's personal or inward response in encounter with the paradox as a historical reality as opposed to being a contradiction.

In the same manner, he poses the God-freedom paradox as a problem of inner appropriation. Without overlooking the objectivity and the dichotomy of its relation, he stresses the problem demands inward response.

A way to understand the mystery of the relation between God and humanity as such does not lie within the intellect alone. According to Kierkegaard, subjectivity (inward appropriation) is the only alternative to appropriating the eternal-historical paradox, the intersecting boundary between God and history. His point is the truth of God-freedom relation resides within the subject. The problem is subjective, and thus it demands a subjective solution.

According to both Kierkegaard and Barth, the solution to the God-freedom paradox or any other (i.e., faith and reason, love and justice and so on) eternal-historical form of dichotomy does not lie "in the right relation between propositions and historical realities abstractly conceived." Instead, "it must ultimately relate to an existing individual."[63] What the problem seeks is "decision."

What follows from and is related to his claim—the subjectivity of God-freedom relation—is the transcendent as an absolute other. God, who is the absolute other, lies outside time. He is wholly other who stands over and against history. Thus the solution to any historical problem with respect to the transcendent cannot be answered objectively outside the eternal subject.

The solution to the God-freedom problem then is to be thought in the context of subjectivity and God as the wholly other. The problem demands choice. It demands decision of faith over and against proof. It demands our will to believe.

Kierkegaard's insistence that truth is subjectivity emphasizes that truth is ultimately personal. Truth does not "hang in the air"; it resides in an existing subject. It follows from this that God, for Kierkegaard, is not given in the will, intellect, or religious consciousness, but as an Other—that is, as an object who is living Subject. God, therefore, is not immanent to any human faculty, but always present as the One who stands over and against us. God is "Wholly Other." If there is any means for relation with the "Wholly Other" God, it is in the moment of "encounter"—an encounter that is a human response made possible by divine initiative."[64]

· 4 ·

CONCLUSION

In this book, I have argued the relation between God and human freedom in Kierkegaard is one of absolute distinction and historical unity which is initiated by God. As much as he separates God and humanity in infinite terms, he conceives historical relation between God and humanity, and thus between God's absolute essence and our historical freedom. He modifies freedom so as to show its limits and how it subjects to God's eternal or absolute initiative.

In that regard, I have argued Kierkegaard's concept of God-freedom relation essentially is linked to God's Incarnation in Jesus Christ. Just as he sees the Incarnation as one of absolute distinction and historical relation, Kierkegaard offers the same solution to the problem of the God-freedom dichotomy, namely as one of qualitative distinction and historical unity.

He contends the relation demands, not so much its theoretical treatment, but an inward appropriation and decision. With respect to the God-freedom dichotomy, one faces the challenge of dialectically qualifying that relation. What materializes the paradox of the God-freedom relation then is an appropriation and decision of faith at the levels of both the eternal and the historical. The aim of each is to achieve unity between God and humanity while seeing their rational contradictions. Human nature is such that it alternates between the eternal and the historical.

Both are irrefutably true: man's independence and his dependence, his freedom and his lack of freedom, his being a self and his being a thing. One cannot cancel either of the conflicting statements without doing harm to the full truth about man. And one cannot mitigate or eliminate the contradiction by dividing the totality of the person into one half that would be free and one half that would be determined. He is alive just in so far as he lives in the tension between the two aspects, ever feeling himself responsible for his decisions and yet also driven to decide as he does. He actually lives within and outside the world, and this contradictory situation generates the consciousness of the bottomless abyss which opens underneath the surface of his existence.[1]

Kierkegaard's concept of unity between the self and the absolute other practically entails the religious pathos of contentment: happiness. Yet one must be mindful that in Kierkegaard the appropriation of the God-freedom paradox limits itself from providing a relative critique. In the world one can only be engaged in an objective or historical undertaking of the problem. Having an absolute truth of the problem of the God-freedom relation on the other hand requires an eternal undertaking. What is required in that pursuit is eternal belief. That belief is given in Jesus.

According to Kierkegaard, "Human beings exist at the crossroad of God's absolute will and their won free will." He declares, "human will is responsible for all of humans' historical and religious life choices"[2] but God is the absolute foundation of our existence. Hence our nature consists of both historical and eternal possibilities. Therefore, history is a strand of free determinations of choices made by human beings. We are also finite beings over whose life God is the absolutely acting cause.[3]

NOTES

Chapter 1: Introduction

1. Tony Kim, *Reasonableness of Faith: A Study of Kierkegaard's Philosophical Fragments* (New York: Peter Lang Publishers Inc., 2012), 120.

2. Louis Pojman, *Kierkegaard's Philosophy of Religion* (San Francisco: International Scholars Publications, 1999), 184.

3. Stephen Evans, *Passionate Reason: Making Sense of Kierkegaard's Philosophical Fragments* (Bloomington: Indiana University Press, 1992), 126.

4. Søren Kierkegaard, *Fear and Trembling and The Book on Adler*, trans. Walter Loweri (New York: Everyman's Library, 1994), 59. Here, we clearly see his concept of revelation as that which stands over and against philosophy (i.e., metaphysics, speculation and so on). He boldly shows his biblical pre-suppositional stand with respect to history and nature. He explores his view further in *Philosophical Fragments* where he explains the truth of the concept by virtue of the logic of stating the argument from being to conclusion of God's being by virtue of seeing the impossibility of arguing from being to existence and vice versa. See Søren Kierkegaard, *Philosophical Fragments*, ed. and trans. Howard V. Hong and Edna H. Hong (Princeton: Princeton University Press, 1985), 39–41.

5. Ibid., 59–60.

6. In a journal entry from 1849, Kierkegaard states: "The man and the ideal are separated from each other in this way. To be so situated as to be able to live for an idea, to be able to employ all one's time for this, is indeed closer to relating oneself to the idea—although, of course, when the ideal is Christ there is the infinite qualitative difference between him

and one [a human being] who comes closest to him." Søren Kierkegaard, *Journals and Papers*, Vol. 1, A-E, ed. and trans. Howard V. Hong and Edna H. Hong (Bloomington: Indiana University Press, 1967), 99.

7. Stephen Evans, "Can God Be Hidden and Evident at the Same Time? Some Kierkegaardian Reflections," Faith *and Philosophy: Journal of the Society of Christian Philosophers* 23, no. 3 (July 2006): 241–52 (especially 242–43).

8. Paul Tillich, *Systematic Theology*, Vol. I (Chicago: The University of Chicago Press, 1951), 201.

Chapter 2: Modern Concepts of Freedom

1. Martin Heidegger, *The Essence of Human Freedom: An Introduction to Philosophy*, trans. Ted Sadler (London: Continuum, 2002), 16.
2. Ibid.
3. Immanuel Kant, *Critique of Pure Reason*, trans. Werner S. Pluhar (Indianapolis: Hackett Publishing Company Inc., 1996), 327.
4. Ibid., 150–51.
5. Stephan Körner, *Kant* (Baltimore: Penguin Books Inc., 1967), 91.
6. Ibid., 93.
7. Ibid., 93–4.
8. Here what distinguishes Kierkegaard from Kant is the unscientific presupposition in which his metaphysics is rooted. Unlike Kant, who says that one hypothetically presupposes God's existence each time one performs a moral act, Kierkegaard's metaphysics is grounded in the historical relation between God and human knowledge.

   According to Kierkegaard, every human being lives with historical or natural concept or knowledge of the transcendent. One is aware of the transcendent apart from living morally.
9. Körner, *Kant*, 94.
10. Ibid.
11. Ibid., 94–5.
12. *Pure Reason*, 29–30.
13. Immanuel Kant, *Critique of Practical Reason*, ed. and trans. Lewis White Beck (Upper Saddle River: Prentice Hall), 17.
14. Immanuel Kant, *Groundwork of the Metaphysics of Morals*, ed. and trans. Mary Gregor (Cambridge: Cambridge University Press, 1997), 57.
15. Ibid.
16. Karl Jaspers, *Kant*, ed. Hannah Arendt, trans. Ralph Manheim (New York: A Harvard Book, 1957), p. 65.
17. Ibid.
18. Immanuel Kant, *Lectures on Philosophical Theology*, trans. Allen Wood and Gertrude M. Clark (Ithaca: Cornell University Press, 1978), 122.
19. Immanuel Kant, *Political Writings*, ed. H. S. Reiss, trans. H. B. Nisbet (Cambridge: Cambridge University Press, 1991), 185.

20. Heidegger, *Human Freedom*, 16–7. There, Heidegger correctly notes that Kant makes distinction between cosmological freedom and practical freedom. According to Heidegger, Kant conceives cosmological freedom as "the power of beginning a state spontaneously." He says that "Such causality will not, therefore, itself stand under another cause determining it in time, as required by the law of nature." "Freedom in this sense," he says, "is a pure transcendental idea" and "Freedom, therefore, is the power of the self-origination of a state" in Kant. By practical freedom, says Heidegger, Kant means "the will's independence of coercion through sensuous impulses." The practical concept of freedom in Kant, he notes, refers to its independence. It points to independence as it was characterized before, namely, negative freedom. It is freedom that is independent which does not rely on another source.

21. Reinhold Neibuhr, *The Nature and Destiny of Man: A Christian Interpretation*, Volume 1 (New York: Charles Scribner's Sons, 1964), 145.

22. In his early work, *The One Possible Basis for a Demonstration of God*, Kant rationally shows God's existence as a necessity without relevance to the world. He calls God's existence "an element of reality." On the basis of that hypothetical recognition of God as an element of reality he attempts to show systematic demonstration of God's being.

23. Immanuel Kant, *The One Possible Basis for a Demonstration of the Existence of God*, trans. Gordon Treash (Nebreska: University of Nebreska Press, 1979), 119.

24. Karl Barth, *Protestant Theology in the Nineteenth Century: Its Background and History* (Grand Rapids: William Eerdmans Publishing Company, 2002), 23–4.

25. Daniel J. Price, *Karl Barth's Anthropology in Light of Modern Thought* (Grand Rapids: William Eerdmans Publishing Company, 2002), 37–8.

26. Kant defines transcendental deduction as a way of determining how "concepts can refer to objects a priori." Those concepts he calls: "determined for pure a priori use." Kant, *Pure Reason*, 142.

27. Ibid., 146.

28. Anthony Rudd, "Speculation and Despair: Metaphysical and Existential Perspectives on Freedom," *Kierkegaard and Freedom* (New York: Palgrave Publishers, 2000), 28.

29. Ibid.

30. Ibid., 33.

31. Ibid., 34.

32. Ibid., 34.

33. Ibid., 36.

34. Søren Kierkegaard's Journals and Papers, Vol. 2., ed. and trans. Howard V. Hong and Edna H. Hong (Indiana University Presss, Bloomington), 1970, 165.

35. Patricia J. Huntington, "Heidegger's Reading of Kierkegaard Revisited: From Ontological Abstraction to Ethical Concretion," *Kierkegaard in Post/Modernity*, ed. Martin J. Matustik and Merold Westphal (Bloomington: Indiana University Press, 1995), 43.

36. Heidegger, *Human Freedom*, 4.

37. Ibid. Heidegger gives two definitions of human freedom. One is the negative concept, which is defined as independence; and the second is the positive concept of human freedom, which he says was the main concern of Kant with respect to the meaning of the essence of human freedom.

38. Ibid., 15.

39. Ibid.

40. Ibid.

41. Ibid.

42. Ibid., 4–5. Here, Heidegger uses the term "God" purely in a hypothetical way. His stance against religion is one of non-commitment.

43. Ibid., 5.

44. Ibid.

45. Michael Wyschgrod, *Kierkegaard and Heidegger: The Ontology of Experience* (New York: Humanities Press, 1969), 37.

46. Ibid. 37–8.

47. Ibid., 38. The central position of freedom in Kierkegaard thus becomes apparent. It would not be understanding it, however, if the characteristically existential nature of it were not made clear. For a non-existential understanding freedom is usually a determinant that enters a situation in which the factors are already given and what remains is the exercise of freedom with regard to them.

48. Martin Heidegger, *Being and Time*, trans. John Macquarrie and Edward Robinson (New York: Harper-Collins Publishers, 1962), 1.

49. Ibid., 374.

50. Wyschgrod, *Kierkegaard and Heidegger*, 38.

51. Søren Kierkegaard, *Concluding Unscientific Postscript to the Philosophical Fragments*, trans. Howard V. Hong and Edna H. Hong (Princeton: Princeton University, 1992), 35.

52. Kim, *Reasonableness*, 35.

53. Tillich, *Systematic*, 214–15.

54. Ibid, 215.

55. Ibid., 184.

56. Ibid. See the footnote.

57. Ibid.

58. Ibid.

59. Ibid., 183

60. Ibid.

61. Jolita Pons, *Stealing a Gift: Kierkegaard's Pseudonyms and the Bible* (New York: Fordham University Press, 2004), xi.

62. L. Joseph Rosas III, *Scripture in the Thought of Søren Kierkegaard* (Nashville: Broadman and Holman Publishers, 1994), 46.

63. Ibid., 39.

64. Stanley Cavell, "Kierkegaard's On Authority and Authenticity," *Soren Kierkegaard: Critical Assessments of Leading Philosophers*, Volume 1. Authority and Authenticity: Kierkegaard and His Pseudonyms (London: Routledge, 2002), 37–38.

65. Ibid., 38.

66. Norman Lillegard, "Revelation, Interpretation, Authority," *Hermeneutics at the Crossroads*, ed. Kevin J. Vanhoozer, James K. A. Smith, Bruce Ellis Benson (Bloomington: Indiana University Press, 2006).

67. Ibid.

68. Ibid.

69. Ibid.

70. Ibid.

71. Ibid., 39.

72. Ibid., 37–8.

73. John Elrod, *Being and Existence in Kierkegaard's Pseudonymous Works* (Princeton: Princeton University Press, 1975), 13.

74. William L. McBride, "Sartre's Debts to Kierkegaard: A Partial Reckoning," *Kierkegaard in Post/Modernity*, ed. Martin J. Matustik and Merold Westphal (Bloomington and Indianapolis: Indiana University Press, 1995), 19.

75. Ibid., 18.

76. Ibid.

77. Manuela Hackel, Jean-Paul Sartre: Kierkegaard's Influence on His Theory of Nothingness," *Kierkegaard and Existentialism*, Kierkegaard Research: Sources, Reception and Resources, Vol. 9, ed. Jon Stewart (Burlington: Ashgate Publishing Company, 2011), 332.

78. Ibid., 332–33.

79. Ibid., 333.

80. Ibid., 323.

81. Ibid., 333.

82. Ibid., 332.

83. Betty Cannon, *Sartre & Psychoanalysis: An Existentialist Challenge to Clinical Metatheory* (Kansas: University Press of Kansas, 1991), 4.

84. Majori Grene, *Sartre* (New York: New Viewpoints, 1973), 92.

85. Ibid., 94.

86. Ibid., 93.

87. Ibid.

88. Evans, *Passionate Reason*, 27.

89. Grene, 84–5.

90. Ibid., 84.

91. Ibid., 85.

92. Ibid., 86.

93. Pons, *Stealing*, xii.

94. Ibid.

95. For example, Stanley Cavell in his "Kierkegaard's On Authority and Revelation" argues that the often uttered phrase that Kierkegaard is a "profound psychologist" is often a misleading aggrandizement. Although this is not untrue, Cavell argues that what is profound psychology in the philosopher is none other than the faith he holds, namely Christianity, and as such must be perceived as grounding his psychological concepts on his deep understanding of the Christian doctrines and experience. See Stanley Cavell, "Kierkegaard On Authority and Revelation," *Søren Kierkegaard: Critical Assessments of Leading Philosophers*, Volume 1. *Authorship and Authenticity: Kierkegaard and His Pseudonyms*, ed. Daniel W. Conway with K. E. Gover (London: Routledge, 2001), 41.

96. Ibid., xiii.

97. Ibid.

98. Hermann Deuser, "Religious Dialectics and Christology," *The Cambridge Companion to Kierkegaard*, ed. Alastair Hannay and Gordon D. Marino (Cambridge: Cambridge University Press, 1997), 378–79.

19. In *Bondage of the Will*, Luther writes: "For what is sought by means of free choice is to make room for merits.

100. Søren Kierkegaard, *The Present Age*, trans. Alexander Dru (New York: Harper & Row Publishers, 1962), 33.

101. Richard Kroner, *Culture and Faith* (Chicago: The University of Chicago Press, 1951), 26.

102. Ibid., 19.

103. Ibid.

104. Ibid.

105. Ibid., 19–20.

106. Ibid., 20.

107. Jon Stewart, *Kierkegaard's Relation to Hegel Reconsidered* (Cambridge: Cambridge University Press, 2003), 484.

108. Ibid.

109. Ibid.

110. Peter C. Hodgson, *Hegel and Christian Theology: A Reading of the Lectures on the Philosophy of Religion* (Oxford: Oxford University Press, 2005), 107.

111. Ibid., 115.

112. Emil L. Fackenheim, *The Religious Dimensions of Hegel's Thought* (Bloomington: Indiana University Press, 1967), 16.

113. Ibid.

114. Pons, *Stealing*, 56.

115. Ibid.

116. Ibid.

117. Hent De Vries, *Religion and Violence: Philosophical Perspectives from Kant to Derrida* (Baltimore: The Johns Hopkins University Press, 2002), 139.

118. Walter Kaufman, *Hegel: A Reinterpretation* (Notre Dame: University of Notre Dame Press, 1965), 237.

119. Ibid.

120. Brian Hebblethwaite, *Philosophical Theology and Christian Doctrine*, ed. Michael L. Peterson (Malden: Blackwell Publishers), 38.

121. Quoted from Terry Pinkard, *German Idealism 1760–1860: The Legacy of Idealism* (Cambridge: Cambridge University Press, 2002), 346.

122. William Desmond, *Hegel's God: A Counterfeit Double* (Burlington: Ashgate Publishing Company, 2003), 6.

123. Kierkegaard, *Fragments*, 78. Climacus quotes Hegel's explanation from his *Science of Logic* as a way of affirming his view of Hegel's philosophy as nothing more than an invention, a play of the mind: From this course the method has emerged as the self-knowing Notion that has itself, as the absolute, both subjective and objective, *for its subject matter*, consequently as the pure correspondence of the Notion and its reality, as a concrete existence that is the Notion itself. Accordingly, what is to be considered here as method is only the movement of the *Notion* itself, the nature of which movement has already been cognized;

but *first*, there is now the added *significance* that the *Notion is everything*, and its movement is the *universal absolute activity*, the self-determining and self-realizing movement. The method is therefore to be recognized as the unrestrictedly universal, internal and external mode; and as the absolutely infinite force, to which no object, presenting itself as something external, remote from and independent of reason, could offer resistance or be of a particular nature in opposition to it, or could not be penetrated by it. It is therefore *soul and substance*, and anything whatever is comprehended and known in its truth only when it is completely *subjugated to the method*; it is the method proper to every subject matter because its activity is the Notion. This is also the truer meaning of its universality; according to the universality of reflection it is regarded merely as the method for *everything*; but according to the universality of the Idea, it is both the manner peculiar to cognition, to the *subjectively* self-knowing Notion, and also the objective manner, or *reflection as others*. It is therefore not only the highest *force*, or rather the *sole* and absolute *force* or reason, but also its supreme and sole *urge* to find and cognize *itself by means of itself in everything*.

124. Hans Küng, *The Incarnation of God: An Introduction to Hegel's Theological Thought as Prolegomena to a Future Christology*, trans. J. R. Stephenson (New York: The Crossroad Publishing Company, 1970), 128.

125. Ibid.

126. Dale M. Schlitt, *Hegel's Trinitarian Claim: A Critical Reflection* (Leiden: E. J. Brill, 1984), 11.

127. Søren Kierkegaard, *Training in Christianity*, ed. and trans. Howard V. Hong and Edna H. Hong (Princeton: Princeton University Press, 1991), 127.

128. Gregor Malanschuk, *Kierkegaard's Concept of Existence*, ed. and trans. Howard V. Hong and Edna H. Hong (Milwaukee: Marquette University Press, 2003), 18.

129. Ibid., 18–9.

130. Ibid.

131. In referring to all rational categories, he writes:

Not even one of the categories can we define really, i.e., make understandable the possibility of its object, without immediately descending to conditions of sensibility and hence to the form of appearances; to these appearances, as their sole objects, the categories must consequently be limited. For if we take away the mentioned condition, then all signification, i.e., reference to the object, is gone; and through no example can we then make comprehensible to ourselves just what sort of thing is in fact meant by such a concept. Kant, *Pure Reason*, 306–07.

132. John Morrison, "Christ, Faith, and the Problem of History in the Thought of Soren Kierkegaard," *Philosophi Christi*, Journal of Evangelical Philosophical Society, Vol. 18:2, 1995, 16.

133. Kierkegaard, *Fragments*, 37.

134. Sytse U. Zuidema, *Kierkegaard*, trans. David H. Freeman (Philadelphia: Presbyterian and Reformed Publishing Co., 1960), 34.

135. Ibid., 35.

136. In *Postscript* Kierkegaard writes: "The way of objective reflection makes the subject accidental, and thereby transforms existence into something indifferent, something vanishing…It

leads to abstract thought, to mathematics, to historical knowledge of different kinds; and from the objective point of view quite rightly, becomes infinitely indifferent." Kierkegaard, *Postscript*, 193.

137. Robert L. Perkins, "Introduction," *International Kierkegaard Commentary*, ed. Robert L. Perkins (Macon: Mercer University Press, 1994), 10.

138. John Wild, "Kierkegaard and Contemporary Existentialist Philosophy," *A Kierkegaard Critique*, ed. Howard A. Johnson and Neils Thulstrup (Chicago: Henry Regnery Company, 1962), 23–4.

139. Helmut Thielicke, *Modern Faith & Thought*, trans. Geoffery W. Bromley (Grand Rapids: William B. Eerdman Publishing Company, 1990), 494.

140. G. W. F. Hegel, *Phenomenology of Spirit*, trans. A. V. Miller (Oxford: Oxford University Press, 1979), 120.

141. Lee M. Capel, "Historical Introduction," *The Concept of Irony with Constant Reference to Socrates* (New York: Harper & Row, Publishers, 1965), 34.

142. Ibid., 34–5.

143. Ibid., 35.

144. Ibid.

145. Ibid.

146. Ibid.

147. Capel also holds this view. He writes: "This much of his clarified experience Kierkegaard is concerned to communicate in the essay on irony, and this note of tempered humanism abides as the authentic seriousness of the work—the true point of departure for his subsequent 'authorship.'" Capel, "Historical Introduction," 36.

Chapter 3: Unity of Faith and Reason

1. Timothy P. Jackson, "Arminian Edification: Kierkegaard on Grace and Free Will," *The Cambridge Companion to Kierkegaard*, ed. Alastair Hannay and Gordon D. Marion (Cambridge: Cambridge University Press, 1998), 237.

2. Ibid., 238.

3. Ibid., 239.

4. Ibid., 240.

5. Ibid.

6. Ibid., 241.

7. Ibid., 241.

8. Ibid., 247.

9. Kierkegaard, *Fragments*, 15.

10. Kim, *Reasonableness*, 29–30.

11. Søren Kierkegaard, *For Self-Examination*, trans. and ed. Howard V. Hong and Edna H. Hong (Princeton: Princeton University Press, 1990), 16.

12. Ibid., 16–17. The fact that Luther gave primacy to faith over and against works is expressed in the words of Heinrich Boehmer in his *Martin Luther: Road to Reformation*, where Luther's view with respect to the God-humanity/freedom relation as one of absolute

distinction and historical unity is indirectly depicted by Luther against his opponent (Roman Church) concerning indulgence: "in view of this conflict of opinions, Luther felt the urgent necessity of preparing an authentic statement to expound the true meaning of his 'paradoxes.' About the beginning of February, 1518, he was able to submit these explanations of the Ninety-five Theses to his diocesan with request that he ruthlessly strikeout everything in them that appeared offensive to him; For 'I know that Christ does not need me. He will show His church what is good for her without me.'

13. Ibid., 17.

14. Søren Kierkegaard, *Works of Love*, ed. and trans. Howard V. Hong and Edna H. Hong (Princeton: Princeton University Press, 1995), 19.

15. Ibid., 269.

16. Ibid., 147.

17. Dietrich Bonhoeffer, *Letters and Papers*, Works, Vol. 8, ed. John W. De Gruchy, trans. Barbara and Martin Rumscheidt (Minneapolis: Fortress Press, 2010), 501.

18. Here, Kierkegaard is in accord, for example, with John Calvin who says that a person is always aware of the being of God. Calvin further states one is aware or has the knowledge of God as the creator, and the judge of humanity. He says human beings live with a certain sense of guilt and expectation of God's accorded judgment on them for their sinful existence. His statement here is in accord with Kierkegaard as far as what he writes in his work *The Concept of Anxiety*, for instance, where he treats the problem of sin as an ongoing condition of human existence.

19. Daniel J. Price, *Karl Barth's Anthropology in Light of Modern Thought* (Grand Rapids: William B. Eerdmans Publishing Company, 2002), 86.

20. Ibid.

21. Kant, *Pure Reason*, 157.

22. Ibid.

23. One place among many works where his unprejudiced thought, from either side of the viewpoint of faith and reason, is demonstrated is his book, *Transcendental Problems of Theoretical Thought*. There, Dooyeweerd writes: "I do not pretend that my transcendental investigation should be unprejudiced. The really critical character of my transcendental method appears only from its sharp distinction between theoretic judgments and super-theoretic [religious] prejudices and from its merciless fighting against the current dogmatic confusions of both of these behind the mask of an 'autonomous' science. However, the results of my inquiry are not implied in my starting point. If this were true, it would seem a little astonishing that Christian thought has not detected long ago the *inner point of connection* between religion and scientific theory. This point of connection could only be discovered by means of a serious thought itself. And this is a matter of critical *science*, not a matter of *dogmatic confession*." Herman Dooyeweerd, *Transcendental Problems of Theoretical Thought* (Grand Rapids: W.M.B. Eerdmans Publishing Company, 1948), vi.

24. Paul Tillich, *Dynamics of Faith* (New York: Harper & Row Publishers, 1957), 76–7. Emphasis is mine.

25. Emmanuel Levinas, "A Propos of Kierkegaard Vivant," *Soren Kierkegaard: Critical Assessment of Leading Philosophers*, Volume 1, Authorship and Authenticity: Kierkegaard and His Pseudonyms, ed. Daniel W. Conway and K. E. Gover (London: Routledge, 2002), 113–14.

26. For a detailed discussion on this topic see Stanley Cavell, *Kierkegaard's 'On Authority and Revelation,'* 37–50.
27. For example, natural and human sciences play an important role in adding objective contribution to the validity of Christian faith in Kierkegaard.
28. Merold Westphal, "Kierkegaard on Language and Spirit," *Language and Spirit*, ed. D. Z. Phillips and Mario Von Der Ruhr (Basingstoke: Macmillan Distribution L.T.D., 2004), 65.
29. According to Ricoeur scholar Erazim Kohák, for Ricoeur "The reasons which motivate my decision, the body which I am, even the personal and historical conditions of my being are not simply external limitations imposed upon me, but rather the organ in and through which I am actual. I am not identical with them, yet I am at all only through them and in them. While my freedom is actual only in and through my nature, the voluntary only by reason of the involuntary, that very 'nature,' that involuntary, becomes meaningful only in relation to the Cogito incarnate in and through it. Whatever may or may not be the case means nothing unless an 'I' appropriates it as the motive of decision, as the organ of action, and as the condition of its being. Husserl's use of the Greek term *hyle* describes it quite appropriately: it is my freedom which transforms it into a meaningful 'nature' while it itself becomes actual through it." See Paul Ricoeur, *Freedom and Nature: The Voluntary and the Involuntary*, trans. Erazim V. Kohák (Evanston: Northwestern University Press, 2007), xix–xx.
30. In Kierkegaard, this relation takes place in time and uncovers its transcendent origin and determination in God in our consciousness.
31. Kant, *Pure Reason*, 91.
32. Ibid.
33. Kierkegaard, *Fragments*, 75.
34. Ibid.
35. Ibid., 77.
36. Ibid.
37. Ibid., 78.
38. Ibid., 74.
39. Elrod, *Being and Existence*, 54.
40. Kierkegaard, *Fragments*, 74. In *Fragments*, Climacus points out that we also find this historically formulated notion of human freedom in Aristotle, whose influence on Hegel cannot be denied. Climacus critically writes:
    (Aristotle's theory of two kinds of the possible in relation to the necessary). His mistake is to begin with the thesis that everything necessary is possible. To avoid contradictory—indeed, self-contradictory—statements about the necessary, he makes shift by formulating two kinds of the possible instead of discovering that his first thesis is incorrect, since the possible cannot be predicted to the necessary. The change of coming into existence is actuality, the transition takes place in freedom. No coming into existence is necessary—not before it comes into existence, for then it cannot come into existence, and not after it has come into existence, for then it has not come into existence. See 74–5.
41. Malanschuk, *Kierkegaard's Concept*, 19.

42. Like Kierkegaard and Heidegger, Sartre also ponders that concept. According to Sartre, human moods such as anxiety, despair and so on form the structural foundation of human existence. They are the base of our being. According to Sartre, existence precedes essence. That means one can determine in terms of how he or she wants to be determined, how one wants to be shaped as a human being. We are what we make of ourselves at the end. The fact that we as human beings can do that implies freedom. According to Sartre, human beings are not bound to options. They are not bound to necessity. He says to think we have an option prior to taking action implies necessity, since that means the choice made is the right and necessary one among others. Necessity, he says, is same as impossibility. It means absence or lack of freedom. That equals to: human beings are not free; they are inauthentic, as it were.
43. Kierkegaard, *Fragments*, 37.
44. Zuidema, *Kierkegaard*, 34.
45. Ibid., 52.
46. Kierkegaard, *Fragments*, 50.
47. Kim, *Reasonableness*, 54.
48. Ibid.
49. Ibid.
50. Ibid.
51. Ibid.
52. Ibid., 52–3.
53. Ibid., 53.
54. Ibid.
55. Price, *Barth*, 87.
56. Ibid.
57. Ibid.
58. Ibid.
59. Ibid., 87–8.
60. Karl Barth, *Church Dogmatics*, Vol. III: The Doctrine of Creation, Part I, trans. J. W. Edwards and, O. Bussey (Peabody: Hendrickson Publications, 2010), vii.
61. Kierkegaard, *Journals*, V.1. 125.
62. Ibid., 29.

63. Price, *Barth*, 88.
64. Ibid.

Chapter 4: Conclusion

1. Kroner, *Culture*, 48.
2. Kim, *Reasonableness*, 110.
3. Evans, *Passionate Reason*, 126.

BIBLIOGRAPHY

Works by or on Søren Kierkegaard

Capel, Lee M. *The Concept of Irony with Constant Reference to Socrates*. New York: Harper & Row Publishers, 1965.

Cavell, Stanley. "Kierkegaard's On Authority and Authenticity." *Soren Kierkegaard: Critical Assessment of Leading Philosophers*, Vol. I. Edited by Daniel Conway and K. E. Gover. London: Routledge, 2002.

Deuser, Hermann. "Religious Dialectics and Christology." *The Cambridge Companion to Kierkegaard*. Edited by Alastair Hannay and Gordon D. Marino. Cambridge: Cambridge University Press, 1997.

Elrod, John. *Being and Existence in Kierkegaard's Pseudonymous Works*. Princeton: Princeton University Press, 1975.

Evans, Stephen. "Can God be Hidden and Evident at the Same Time? Some Kierkegaardian Reflections." *Faith and Philosophy: Journal of the Society of Christian Philosophers* 23, no. 3 (2006): 241–252.

———. *Passionate Reason: Making Sense of Kierkegaard's Philosophical Fragments*. Bloomington: Indiana University Press, 1992.

Hackel, Manuela. "Jean-Paul Sartre: Kierkegaard's Influence on his Theory of Nothingness." *Kierkegaard and Existentialism*. Kierkegaard Research: Sources, Reception and Resources. Vol. 9. Edited by Jon Stewart. Burlington: Ashgate Publishing Company, 2011.

Jackson, Timothy P. "Arminian Edification: Kierkegaard on Grace and Free Will." *The Cambridge Companion to Kierkegaard.* Edited by Alastaire Hannay and Gordon D. Marion. Cambridge: Cambridge University Press, 1998.

Kierkegaard, Soren. *Concluding Unscientific Postscript to the Philosophical Fragments.* Edited and Translated by Howard V. Hong and Edna H. Hong. Princeton: Princeton University Press, 1992.

————. *Fear and Trembling and The Book on Adler.* Translated by Walter Loweri. New York: Everyman's Library, 1994.

————. *For Self-Examination.* Edited and translated by Howard V. Hong and Edna H. Hong. Princeton: Princeton University Press, 1990.

————. *Journals and Papers.* Edited and translated by Howard V. Hong and Edna H. Hong. Vol. 1. Princeton: Princeton University Press, 1967.

————. *Philosophical Fragments.* Edited and translated by Howard V. Hong and Edna H. Hong. Princeton: Princeton University Press, 1985.

————. *The Present Age.* Translated by Alexander Dru. New York: Harper & Row Publishers, 1962.

————. *Training in Christianity.* Edited and translated by Howard V. Hong and Edna H. Hong. Princeton: Princeton University Press, 1991.

————. *Works of Love.* Edited and translated by Howard V. Hong and Edna H. Hong. Princeton: Princeton University Press, 1995.

Kim, Tony. *Reasonableness of Faith: A Study of Kierkegaard's Philosophical Fragments.* New York: Peter Lang, 2012.

Levinas, Emmanuel. "A Propos Kierkegaard Vivant." *Soren Kierkegaard: Critical Assessment of Leading Philosophers.* Vol. 1. Authorship and Authenticity: Kierkegaard and His Pseudonyms. Edited by Daniel W. Conway and K. E. Gover. London: Routledge, 2002.

Lillegard, Norman. "(Revelation, Interpretation) Authority." *Hermeneutics at the Crossroads.* Edited by Kevin J. Vanhoozer. Bloomington: Indiana University Press, 2006.

Malantschuk, Gregor. *Kierkegaard's Concept of Existence.* Edited and translated by Howard V. Hong and Edna H. Hong. Milwaukee: Marquette University Press, 2003.

Mcbride, William L. "Sartre's Debts to Kierkegaard: A Partial Reckoning." *Kierkegaard in Post/ Modernity.* Edited by Martin J. Mastuštic and Merold Westphal. Bloomington: Indiana University Press, 1995.

Morrison, John. "Christ, Faith, and the Problem of History in the Thought of Soren Kierkegaard." *Philosophia Christi: Journal of Evangelical Philosophical Society* 18, no. 2 (1995): 15–41.

Perkins, Robert L. "Introduction." *International Kierkegaard Commentary.* Edited by Robert L. Perkins. Macon: Mercer University Press, 1994.

Pojman, Louis. *Kierkegaard's Philosophy of Religion.* San Francisco: International Scholars Publication, 1999.

Pons, Jolita. *Stealing a Gift: Kierkegaard's Pseudonyms and the Bible.* New York: Fordham University Press, 2004.

Rosas, L. Joseph. *Scripture in the Thought of Soren Kierkegaard.* Nashville: Broadman and Holman Publishers, 1994.

Rudd, Anthony. "Speculation and Despair: Metaphysical and Existential Perspectives on Freedom." *Kierkegaard and Freedom*. Edited by James Giles. New York: Palgrave Publishers, 2000.

Stewart, Jon. *Kierkegaard's Relations to Hegel Reconsidered*. Cambridge: Cambridge University Press, 2003.

Westphal, Merold. "Kierkegaard on Language and Spirit." *Language and Spirit*. Edited by D. Z. Phillips and Mario Von Der Ruhr. Basingstoke: Mcmillan Distribution L. T. D., 2004.

Wild, John. "Kierkegaard and Contemporary Existentialist Philosophy." *A Kierkegaard Critique*. Edited by Howard A. Johnson and Neils Thulstrup. Chicago: Henry Regnery Company, 1962.

Zuidema, Sytse U. *Kierkegaard*. Translated by David H. Freeman. Philadelphia: Presbyterian and Reformed Publishing Co., 1960.

Other Works

Barth, Karl. *Church Dogmatics*. Vol. III. The Doctrine of Creation. Part I. Translated by J. W. Edwards and O. Bussey. Edited by G. W. Bromiley and T. F. Torrance. Peabody: Hendrickson Publishers, 2010.

———. *Protestant Theology in the Nineteenth Century: Its Background and History*. Grand Rapids: William Eerdmans Publishing Company, 2002.

Bonhoeffer, Deitrich. "Letters and Papers." *Works*, Vol. 8. Translated by Barbara and Martin Rumscheidt. Edited by John W. De Gruchy. Minneapolis: Fortress Press, 2010.

Cannon, Betty. *Sartre & Psychoanalysis: An Existentialist Challenge to Clinical Metatheory*. Kansas: University Press of Kansas, 1991.

Desmond, William. *Hegel's God: A Counterfeit Double?* Hampshire: Ashgate Publishing Limited Gower House, 2003.

De Vries, Hent. *Religion and Violence: Philosophical Perspectives from Kant to Derrida*. Baltimore: The Johns Hopkins University Press, 2002.

Dooyeweerd, Herman. *Transcendental Problems of Theoretical Thought*. W.M.B. Eerdman Publishing Company, 1948.

Fackenheim, Emil L. *The Religious Dimensions of Hegel's Thought*. Bloomington: Indiana University Press, 1967.

Grene, Marjorie. *Sartre*. New York: New Viewpoints, 1973.

Habblethwaite, Brian. *Philosophical Theology and Christian Doctrine*. Edited by Michael L. Peterson. Malden: Blackwell Publishers, 2005.

Hegel, G. W. F. *Phenomenology of Spirit*. Translated by A. V. Miller. Oxford: Oxford University Press, 1979.

Heidegger, Martin. *The Essence of Human Freedom*. Translated by Ted Sadler. London: Continuum, 2002.

———. *Being and Time*. Translated by John Macquarrie and Edward Robinson. New York: Harper-Collins Publishers, 1962.

Huntington, Patricia. "Heidegger's Reading of Kierkegaard Revisited: From Ontological Abstraction to Ethical Concretion." *Kierkegaard in Post/Modernity.* Edited by Martin J. Matuštik and Merold Westphal. Bloomington: Indiana University Press, 1995.

Hodgson, Peter C. *Hegel and Christian Theology: A Reading of the Lectures on the Philosophy of Religion.* Oxford: Oxford University Press, 2005.

Jasper, Karl. *Kant.* Translated by Ralph Manheim. Edited by Hannah Arendt. New York: A Harvard Book, 1957.

Kant, Immanuel. *Critique of Practical Reason.* Edited and translated by Lewis White Beck. Upper Saddle River: Prentice Hall, 1993.

————. *Critique of Pure Reason.* Translated by Werner S. Pluhar. Indianapolis: Hackett Publishing Company Inc., 1996.

————. *Groundwork of the Metaphysics of Morals.* Edited and translated by Mary Gregor. Cambridge: Cambridge University Press, 1997.

————. *Lectures on Philosophical Theology.* Translated by Allen Wood and Gertrude M. Clark. Ithaca: Cornell University Press, 1978.

————. *Political Writings.* Translated by H. B. Nisbet. Edited by H. S. Reiss. Cambridge: Cambridge University Press, 1991.

————. *The One Possible Basis for a Demonstration of the Existence of God.* Translated by Gordon Treash. Nebreska: University of Nebreska Press, 1979.

Kaufmann, Walter. *Hegel: A Reinterpretation.* Notre Dame: The University of Notre Dame Press, 1965.

Körner, Stephan. *Kant.* Baltimore: Penguin Books Inc., 1967.

Kroner, Richard. *Culture and Faith.* Chicago: The University of Chicago Press, 1951.

Küng, Hans. *The Incarnation of God: An Introduction to Hegel's Theological Thought as Prolegomena to a Future Christology.* Translated by J. R. Stephenson. New York: The Crossroad Publishing Company, 1970.

Michalson, Gordon E. *Kant and the Problem of God.* Massachusetts: Blackwell Publishers, 1999.

Neibuhr, Reinhold. *The Nature and Destiny of Man: A Christian Interpretation.* Vol. 1. New York: Charles Scribner's Sons, 1964.

Pinkard, Terry. *German Idealism 1760–1860: The Legacy of Idealism.* Cambridge: Cambridge University Press, 2002.

Price, Daniel J. *Karl Barth's Anthropology in the Light of Modern Thought.* Grand Rapids: William Eerdmans Publishing Company, 2002.

Ricoeur, Paul. *Freedom and Nature: The Voluntary and the Involuntary.* Translated by Erazim V. Kohák. Evanston: Northwestern University Press, 2007.

Schlitte, Dale M. *Hegel's Trinitarian Claim: A Critical Reflection.* Leiden: E. J. Brill, 1984.

Thielick, Helmut. *Modern Faith & Thought.* Translated by Jeffery W. Bromley. Grand Rapids: William B. Eerdman Publishing Company, 1990.

Tillich, Paul. *Dynamics of Faith.* New York: Harper & Row Publishers, 1957.

————. *Systematic Theology* Vol. 1. Chicago: The University of Chicago Press, 1951.

Wyschgrod, Michael. *Kierkegaard and Heidegger: The Ontology of Experience.* New York: Humanities Press, 1969.

INDEX